Hot Dog Church

and Other Poems from the Pulpit

Troy Tobey

ISBN 978-1-63961-055-6 (paperback)
ISBN 978-1-63961-056-3 (digital)

Copyright © 2021 by Troy Tobey

All rights reserved. No part of this publication may be reproduced, distributed, or transmitted in any form or by any means, including photocopying, recording, or other electronic or mechanical methods without the prior written permission of the publisher. For permission requests, solicit the publisher via the address below.

Christian Faith Publishing
832 Park Avenue
Meadville, PA 16335
www.christianfaithpublishing.com

Printed in the United States of America

I want to dedicate this book to my family in appreciation for all their support and love. Aside from God's bountiful love and grace in my life, my family has been my most treasured blessing! Sharing each day over the past twenty-eight years with my wife Kathleen has been amazing, and she is a constant source of love, joy, and encouragement to me. As well, the journey with my kids Josiah, Lauren, and Micah has been rich and fulfilling beyond all description. Our family adventures have been a catalyst for creativity, humour, and faith-building over the years, and adding Gideon as a son-in-law has made it even more so. In the words of Prison Mike (from *The Office*, US version), "You got a good life!" Yes, we do!

My family on the celebration of our twenty-fifth wedding anniversary

Contents

Introduction 7
A Word If I May 10
Give Us This Day: A Wedding Prayer 12
Dear Old Dad 15
Three Words 17
Shaken, Not Stirred 18
Blame It on Jesus: A Tribute to Charlie Routley 21
There's a New Sheriff in Town 22
Heaven's Bulldozer 24
Can't Sleep 26
Dominoes 28
Red Light! 31
A Healthy Team 33
Hot Dog Church 34
Doormat 36
Finger-paints 38
Ketchup 41
Life Lived in Caps 42
Surfer Psalm (A Surfer's Paraphrase of Psalm 23) 45
Compelling Church 47
Go and Do Likewise 49
The Song 50
Not about Jane 52
An Unfinished Quilt 54
Party in the Barn 56
And They're Off! 57
Neon 59
Ol' Mr. Jones 60
Look to the Son 65
Cream Puff! 68
Walls 71

The Veil	73
A Very Fine Coat	74
Through the Roof	76
This Is A Book	78
My Favourite Things	81
At a Time Like This	83
Tag Team	85
Baggage	87
Super Ball	90
Pirate on Board	92
SOS	95
Bats in the Belfry	96
Blest to Be a Blessing	99
Candy	100
Coach Cliché	102
Pickle	104
A Multitude of Sins	105
The Gospel According to Elvis	107
Father of the Year	108
Fear Not!	111
God-time	115
Picture-Perfect Marriage	117
Could You, Would You?	118
Pierced	120
Grace…and It's Amazing!	123
Heavenly Minded	125
Heaven's Choir	126
Beach Bum	129
Flavour of Canada	131
Last-Minute Shopping Blues	132
Don't Lose Yourself (At the Buffet Table)	135
Go and Make Disciples	137
Harold Will Sleep Tonight	138
No Secret	140
The Last Word	143

Introduction

Words. I've always believed in the power of words. I often quote Proverbs 18:21, "The tongue has the power of life and death, and those who love it will eat its fruit." Words have impact. Words can build up or tear down. Communication can solve or multiply problems.

I guess my love of words and creative writing was there in public school as a child. The odd poem or essay made its way onto a display wall or into a printed publication. But more than that, I developed a love of preaching and the pulpit from a young age, and I soon aspired to be a preacher. And also to play pro-football…but that never worked out. All in all though, I'm glad I went with being a preacher. Probably less bruises than football.

In thirty years of preaching, I've noticed a few things about my approach to the spoken word. A few years back, someone was reviewing a personality assessment test with me, and they noticed my high literary score, so they offhandedly commented, "That means you believe that if you talk about it long enough, you'll solve it." Hmmmm…might explain some of my long sermons!

Although, it was probably never more obvious than when I started as pastor at a new church in 1998 and the normal and predictable one-hour board meetings immediately morphed into three-hour marathons! I wanted everyone to have a chance to speak to every issue, and I suppose somewhere in the back of my mind was an idea—if we talk about it long enough, we will solve it!

Words have power. Over these past thirty years, I've tried many different ways to communicate: sermons, of course, plus newspaper articles, dramatic plays, songs, puppet shows, and even some interpretive dance… although my dance skills are even less impressive than my football skills! Through the years, I've enjoyed speaking in simple poetry, often rhyming couplets that sound like they came out of a Dr. Seuss book. I started tacking a little poem onto the end of a sermon here and there for some oomph, and even at the occasional wedding ceremony for some playful levity. But the most powerful of all quickly became the ones delivered at funerals.

I've chosen the title *Hot Dog Church* because it seems an appropriate metaphor for my approach to ministry: don't be bland! Add garnish and condiments! Within this collection, I've included some pulpit poems on a variety of topics, some fun ditties, even a few songs and parodies. Some were delivered with great emotion or rising dynamics of speed and volume, so much so that several people started asking questions like, "Have you got another *rant* to share with us today?" My end goal and purpose was always to deliver Christian truths in fresh and striking ways that inspire change and stir up spiritual passion. I wholeheartedly agree with the words of one Bible college instructor who told our class, "It is unforgiveable to make the Bible sound boring." And for me, it was cool when someone heard my poem, "Pickle" and told me they'd never look at another pickle without thinking of that poem!

But some of my most cherished titles in this collection are the *life tributes* that were recited at funerals. These represent lives well lived, people I knew and journeyed alongside, and it was my privilege to celebrate their lives in this way. In some cases, people shared their deepest and most personal struggles with me along the way, and on occasion, their final words to me before their passing became the inspiration for the tribute I shared at their funeral. One of my favourite lines is, "Live so the preacher don't hafta lie at your funeral." Ha!

With some of the entries I've included a brief note of explanation or background...often just the tip of the iceberg of all that may be behind the actual words you're reading.

A note of thanks to so many encouraging friends over the years, and to the five congregations we have served in since 1992, especially the crew at Lakeshore Community Church in Bright's Grove, Ontario. Serving as your pastor has been a great joy and a privilege.

Special thanks go to Ramesh Jagoo, for believing this book should be published, and for pushing and prodding at me to make this project a reality...and thanks also for trying to fix my backswing, but my golf game is still terrible!

To the reader: I hope these pages are an enjoyable ride for you, and that you feel blest and inspired as you read on! Oh, it would make me smile to know these words made you laugh a time or two, but I'd so much rather hear you say that these humble words affected you, changed you, encouraged you. That these words impacted you with greater passion for your faith, deeper love for the Lord, and fresh creativity to change the world. After all, that's what words do: words have the power of life…

Sincerely,
Troy Tobey

A Word If I May

A word if I may: I have something to say.
For all my days, this song I raise
As I stand amazed
In the presence of the Nazarene…
Who washed me clean.
I was lost in sin but He intervened.
I owed a debt, but I've been redeemed.
You ask what I have, will it rust or decay?
The world didn't give it and can't take it away!

A word if I may; don't think it cliché,
That the strength of my song is to trust and obey.
Knowing He loves me, stirs up a revelry
Deep within this heart in me.
All glory be unto the Son, the One Who set me free.
Not mere flattery,
But heartfelt sincerity.
What chain can contain my heart's sweet refrain
Of Acclaim for the Name Above all other fame?
Kudos to the Uttermost to the Father, Son and Holy Ghost.
What motivates me? I won't lead you astray—
The world didn't give it, and can't take it away.

A word if I may: sometimes skies are grey.
Whatever the weather, don't be dismayed!
Sometimes it rains and sometimes it pours,
Sometimes you find only closed doors…
But though the wind blows and the thunder roars,
When your heart is renewed and sin's sting is subdued
There's no need for a brooding mood!
Choose an attitude of gratitude.

Wear your heart on your sleeve and your faith display;
The world didn't give it and can't take it away!

A word if I may: time's ticking away.
Surrender your heart and do not delay.
Tick tock, there's the clock;
When it strikes its last and life is past
I'll sing here no more, I'll be on that other shore,
Drawn up higher to a heavenly choir.
And there in that throng I will sing this same song…
That I've been singing all my life long.

In good times and bad, In sad times and glad—
This song is the one thing that I've always had.
How do I manage? Well, I'll tell you how…
I've learned to sing heaven's song right here and now.
What is this song, and how did it start?
God planted the tune in the depths of my heart.

The world didn't give it and can't take it away;
Others may balk it, and mock it, but hey!
This is my story, this is my song… I can praise Jesus, all the day long!

A word if I may: please hear me, I pray.
If you're still staying quiet, today is your day!
The audition for heaven has already begun,
Come join in the song sung for an audience of One.
If you're of this mind, and you don't think it odd…
Give a shout! Let it out! And applaud our great God!
His song is in my heart and forever it will stay,
For the world didn't give it, and can't take it away!

GIVE US THIS DAY
A WEDDING PRAYER

The best thing you can do for someone is pray.
At least that's what I've heard some people say.
So I get on my knees and get right to the task
But what shall I pray…and for what shall I ask?

I could ask God for money and lots of cool stuff…
But just how much stuff would be enough stuff?
If I pray that life is all UPS and no DOWNS,
Would life truly be all SMILES with no FROWNS?

Lord, make life easy, like a summer breeze
And always a sunny 80 degrees.
If there was only one prayer that I could pray
I don't think that would be what I'd say.

If I asked the Lord to keep us healthy and fit,
That would be nice, but that's not quite it.
I know what I'll do… I'll get down and pray…
And ask You dear Lord…give us this day.

Give us this day to live life to the limit
And seize and squeeze each minute that's in it.
From sunrise to midnight and points in between
Just as good and as true as love's ever been.

And as each day ends, as each ended before,
We'll be on our knees, asking for one day more.
One day more to share kisses and wishes and dreams
And laughing and gasping till we burst at the seams.

One more day to share tears, for those shall come too.
Lord we give thanks we can share them with You.
Give us this day whether sunshine or rain.
Give us this day, no matter laughter or pain.

Its true that our lives are not guaranteed,
Just give us this day Lord, that's all that we'll need.
Give us this day, and like all other days
We'll give it right back in glorious praise.

And when our time's finished, and this life is done,
We'll think back on our days…we didn't waste one.
And we will have lived without a regret…
And I'd say that's as good as this life can get.

Note

    I shared this poem at my parents' fiftieth wedding anniversary. It is dedicated to them and the wonderful example of marital love that they have provided to our family and to many more. Marriage truly is lived one day at a time!

My parents, Bill and Donelda, sitting in church
while I preach…and they're both awake!

Dear Old Dad

This is a poem about my dear old dad.
I'm not sure it's fair to compare good dads from bad.
All I know is he's the best dad that I ever had.
And I am glad he is my dad.
I thought I'd share just a brief memory
Of some of the things that my dad means to me.
Please pardon me but I cannot say much
Of his teen years, and childhood and upbringing and such.
For when we first met, he was already grown.
And I can speak only of the dad I have known.
He's been part of my life right from day one.
You probably guessed that since I am his son.
There always were people to see and places to go.
And barns to be cleaned and plowing the snow.
There were chickens to feed and Sunday School too.
Christmas trees and a class trip to the zoo.
Not many dads came on a class trip.
That just goes to show you that my dad was hip.
He once dressed like Santa all red rosy and jolly
And he wore dark-rimmed glasses just like Buddy Holly.
Sometimes with a beard and sometimes without
And if the chores were not done, we would hear him shout!
But of all his great qualities that I think about
It's his caring and helping that really stands out.
In so many times and in so many ways
He's stepped up to help on good and bad days.

Like at my graduation when I got my degree,
I forgot my suit and tie how can this be?
I borrowed a few things, but one thing I lacked,
My dear ol' dad gave me the shirt off his back.

It seems he often comes through in a pinch.
When life throws a curve, he doesn't cower or flinch.
He just steps up and says, "what's wrong?"
Then does his part to help it along.
There once was a time way back when
I thought it was old to be three score and ten.
But my dad sometimes acts like a much younger man.
Offering to help whenever he can.
Giving us rides, or saying a prayer
I am so glad for the times when my dad was there.
Drywall or roofing or automobiles.
And I bet often in spite of the way that he feels.
He's gotten older, and he's showing some wear
So let's treat him gently, and we all best take care.
For whether he's dad or grandpa or brother…
He's quite the palooka, and you won't find another.
One of the nicest fellas you'll ever meet
From the scar on his forehead to the toes on his feet.
I thank the Lord for this blessing I've had
That this dear old fellow is my dear old dad.

Note

My dad, Bill, has always been a tremendous example to me. He did some preaching when I was a kid, and he encouraged me to pursue Christian ministry. This poem was written shortly after he got stitches in his head from a fall (hence the line, "from the scar on his forehead"). He truly did give me the shirt off his back at my college graduation ceremony, and both my parents have been a great support to me throughout my life.

Three Words

Words have the power of life and death.
There are words we love to hear, and words that pierce us deeply.
It doesn't take many words to get a message across.
As little as three words can have powerful impact.
The question is…whose words will you listen to?

The accuser says… You are nothing.
But Jesus says…You are loved.
The accuser says… You don't belong.
Jesus says… You are Mine!
The accuser says… You're a sinner!
Jesus says… You are free!
The accuser says… You are useless!
Jesus says… You are valuable!
The accuser says… This is over. Guilty as charged! We have evidence. You are busted! You're a Loser! No way out. You are through. Bring the chains. Pronounce the verdict. Call it quits. You are finished!

And Jesus says… It is Finished!

Shaken, Not Stirred

The pastor steps up to the pulpit, shaken.
Really shaken, this time. Shaken, not stirred.

Shaken like a dad who just lost his job three weeks before Christmas.
He has a wife, two kids, a mortgage, and a car payment.

Shaken like a woman who just found out about the affair.
Falling apart inside, still she grabs her car keys
And drives the kids to hockey practice, because that's what's written on the calendar.

Shaken like parents who just got a call from the principal.
Drugs at school? Must've been some other kid, they assume…
But it wasn't.

Shaken like a husband who just found out that the cancer is back.
He sits down numbly to make appointments for treatments,
Saying yes to any and every suggested date,
As other schedules suddenly don't matter quite so much anymore.

Shaken like a widow, who just got the final bill from the funeral home.
Came in the mail, same day as the disconnection notice from the power company.
She turns to comment, but sees only an empty chair staring back at her.

The pastor is shaken, as he stands in the pulpit, but not from lack of preparation.
He has his usual ammo of PowerPoint slides, alliterated sermon notes, cross-references and witty anecdotes. He's prayed about this moment too, because that's what good pastors do.

Many times before, he's been stirred… Riled up even.
But now he feels what shaken really is. Shaken, not stirred.
There is a holy terror in his eyes as he looks into the faces of his congregation
And he sees the dad, the woman, the parents, the husband and the widow.
They are all sitting there, waiting to hear from God, not from Coles Notes or a Bible commentary.

He clutches the sides of the sacred desk as perspiration is unleashed all over his body.
Almost overwhelmed, then comes the notion that maybe a weak vessel is exactly what God is looking for…
The notion that God actually *intends* to shake us, not just stir us.
The notion that *until* He shakes us, *unless* He shakes us, like some skin and bones Etch A Sketch,
Can we ever really be all that He has called us to be?

Note

This is a poem I submitted to a writing contest; the topic was "Shaken, Not Stirred." Perhaps they were hoping for words about James Bond, as that was one of his catchphrases? But I wrote about real-life situations in my own congregation at the time, changing a few of the details to protect identities. And yes, I won the prize!

A photo of Charlie and I clasping hands in prayer, not long before he died

Blame It on Jesus
A Tribute to Charlie Routley

What do you say about the inimitable Charlie Routley?
A man who lived out his faith so devoutly?
I'd say blame it on Jesus.
He would shuffle his feet and his eyes would glisten
As he spoke of the Lord to whomever would listen…
Blame it on Jesus, he would say.
In prayer, he was constantly burden bearing…
In evangelism, he was always truth sharing.
In worship, he was forever praise declaring…
In hope, he was never found despairing…
Just go ahead and blame it on Jesus.
In regard to sin, he was a man redeemed.
As to vision, he was a man who dreamed.
In reputation, he was so well esteemed,
And as to his countenance, he simply beamed.
You'll have to blame all that on Jesus.
Charlie knew the credit was not his to claim
He lived for the fame of a greater name.
For all Charlie was and all that he became…
It would be a shame if we did not proclaim…
Blame it on Jesus.

Note

Reverend Charles Routley passed into eternity in 2016, in his ninety-seventh year. He lived with zest for life and love for Jesus, often waving his hands and repeating his trademark phrase, "Blame it on Jesus!" He visited and conducted nursing home church services well into his nineties.

There's a New Sheriff in Town

It was an eerie, dreary, morning in this lonesome little town.
The sun was slowly rising, but no one was around.
They were peeking out their windows, they was huddled behind doors.
They was looking this and that way, they was shakin' in their drawers.

See, their town was on the edge of ruin, it was all fallin' apart.
Every thought was evil, in the deepest of each heart.
Neighbour against neighbour, wicked did abound.
At every corner only lawlessness and evil could be found.

They'd sent word to the governor, please send help right away
We need ourselves a sheriff, who can come and save the day.
The damage must be stopped…and evil must go down…
Spread the word, there's a new sheriff coming to this town.

And all at once, on the horizon, a lonely figure appeared.
He looked a kindly, pleasant man as he slowly neared.
He had no guns or deputies, there was him, and no one else.
How would he turn this town around, all by his lonely self?

People came out to meet him, crawling out from under beds
But who is this, they wondered, all scratching their heads.
We asked for a sheriff of grit, of might and of steel…
But this man seems so gentle, could he be the real deal?

They'd had other sheriffs, but this was not like the rest.
He had no angry scowl, no badge upon his chest.
"I don't need no stinking badge," he said, gentle as a dove.
"I will turn this town around, but I need only truth and love."

The people shouted back, "We want law and order!
Grab lawlessness by its neck and send it 'cross the border.
Every criminal must be herded up and thrown behind bars.
And evil must be banished from this little town of ours!"

But the kindly man said, "Well now, there'd be no one left…
If we locked up everyone guilty of lying, cheating and theft.
You are all guilty, should you all be put away?
Or maybe forgiveness has come to your town today?"

"Sin has ruled here far too long, and evil runs roughshod.
But turn from your wicked ways and give your hearts to God.
You want law and order, but the answer for this place
Is not vigilante justice, but instead, amazing grace."

"Let the Spirit come and change your hearts from the inside out…
And soon you will know what redemption is all about.
You want law and order, you want rights and justice too…
Well now, I'll tell you this, grace is better for you."

"You want things to be different in this little town?
Give your hearts to God, and let His grace abound!
Let His Word soak into your hearts; start to live His way…
God's been waiting for ya, so go ahead…make His day!"

Heaven's Bulldozer

I've tried to be a self-made man.
That with my two hands I could work a plan
I thought I could be strong enough.
If only I could last long enough.
I thought I could bulldoze through it…
I just had to get down and do it.

But every time, my construction
Is hit by delay and interruption.
And I find my best efforts just don't last.
And all too soon I'm out of gas.
The ground won't move beneath my feet.
Finally I agree that I've been beat.
I had given all I've got.
But move an inch? I could not.
There's a mountain in my way.
So punch the clock and call it a day.
Then the Lord says, "I've been watching you.
Do you want to see what I can do?"
You thought you were out of luck.
Nothing would budge, and you were stuck.
But I can help you with this task…
(All you had to do was ask.)
I turned around, the mountain's gone,
(To infinity and beyond.)
With a puzzled look, I scratched my head.
"Not by power, not by might," is what He said.

You thought you could push right through it.
But all your trying could not do it.
The only way through this rock and sod
Is through faith, and by the grace of God.

"Lord, where have you been?" I began to pout.
"Why am I just now finding out?
Who's in on this? Who else knows
That the Lord knows how to bulldoze?"
The Lord said, "I've been here through it all…
All you really had to do was call."

I said, "Thanks, Lord. I've got work to do."
He said, "Hold on: I'm not through with you.
There'll be another mountain tomorrow,
But don't let that cause you any sorrow.
Whenever obstacles seem imposing,
Call on Me, to do bulldozing."
With all my straining at the grindstone,
I cannot do it on my own.
Sometimes it's hard, the path I've chosen:
I need the Lord to do bulldozin'!
There are days when the ground is hard and frozen:
I call out, "Lord—I need bulldozin'!"
The way gets rough, the path gets steep,
The sand gets soft and the muck gets deep.
I cut right through, just like a knife…
When I let the Lord take the wheel of my life.
And when we reach heaven, and there's finally closure…
We'll look back at the tracks of heaven's bulldozer.
And we will know we've arrived at that celestial place…
Not by might, not by power…but by His grace.

Note

    I shared this tribute at my uncle Bud's funeral. He was in construction longer than I can remember, and I recall as a child seeing all his big machinery when we would visit there. I had no idea how much he embraced what God was doing in his life until I visited with him in a cancer ward only weeks before he died. God truly did some amazing things in his life, sometimes with a divine bulldozer!

Can't Sleep

Whatcha gonna do when you can't sleep at night? When you get all uptight because nothing goes right... And the rent is due, and your plans fell through? Well, whatcha gonna do? Flick on a nightlight, and let it shine bright on the Holy Scriptures, and soon you'll get the picture: the Bible gives us all a look at the God of this book.

God is on the throne. You are not alone. You don't have to do it all on your own. He walks right beside you. He will lead and guide you. Under His wings, He will hide you. You have not been lied to: the little bedtime stories about amazing ancient glories are a taste of what He can do in someone just like you when you believe God's Word is true.

And as off to bed you go, something else you need to know: He was with Shadrach and Abednego, and He will be with you also. Joseph was a slave in Egypt, boy did he get ripped! But who could predict that he'd get picked by pharaoh's hand to rule the whole land? I mean, God always comes through...what He did for Joseph, He'll do for you. When it came down to the wire, He was with Hezekiah and Nehemiah and Jeremiah... He'll bring you through the fire. Levi was a far cry from a good man, but God's plan was to set him down and turn him around... Though Levi was a crook, God is the hero of this book!

What God did then, He still does today... So what do you say? Are you going to read the Bible like it's old news? Antiquated views about long-lost Jews, in faraway lands, just singing the blues? Or is it a book of promise and potential, descriptions of the great providential... The God not of yesterday but of tomorrow; the God of joy rather than of sorrow; the God of what could be and what should be. He is the God of possibility, beyond our limited visibility. And in spite of our fragility, by faith God gives ability.

These are not simply fairy tales of apples and arks and very large whales. There is truth in them pages...truth for all the ages.

For both simpletons and sages. The Word is replete with feat after feat, of strength and power in the nick of time and the darkest hour. Worlds were made, foundations laid. Prayers were prayed, debts were paid. Wars were won, and jobs got done. Sinners were saved, the dead were raised, God be praised. Faith extraordinary, like Joseph and like Mary. And then there's Hannah and Anna and crowds singing hosanna. And who's not a fan of sweetest manna, dropping from heaven, all days but the seventh…

Moses goes this trip up Sinai, so why am I so slow to go where God leads me? He feeds me, with faith the size of mustard seeds… that's all I need. That's all it takes to make faith grow. That's what I know; that's what I heard…God is God; so says the Word.

These are canonical chronicles of prodigals and astronomical grace in the face of shame, displaced by love above blame…embracing faith in the name of Jesus…seeping through every line, coming to this heart of mine… Where fear would try to put down root, I'll give it one great big boot, because God gave truth that is absolute, and how can you refute what I know to be absolutely true?

And as I lay me down to sleep, I will slumber in peace so deep. Yes, I will snooze with sweetest sleep; no need for counting little lost sheep. I'm counting promises that God will keep. Thank You, Lord, that I can lay my head upon my bed, knowing faith is alive and fear is dead. Though wind blows and waters rise, though blood red moons fill the skies, though mountains fall and the earth be shook, God is God…so says this book!

DOMINOES

Our whole family got the invite
    To Ruth and Don's one starry night.
Over to their house we goes
    To play a game of Dominoes.
Around the table we all sat.
    And we began to have a chat.
But I think maybe everyone knows
    It's not about the Dominoes.

Everyone wants that double-six…
    And the dominoes fall…with click, click, clicks.
And soon the competition grows…
    But its not really about the dominoes.
Slow but playful goes the pace,
    No furrowed brows or frowning face.
Because as I'm sure everyone knows…
    It's not really about the dominoes.

It's a time to chat and a time to laugh
    And no one cares if you make a gaff.
Unless you play a three on a two
    Ruth would shout, "That you cannot do!"
Life gets hairy, and scary and brutal
    And every effort seems so futile.
Moments when you need some help
    When you cannot do it by yourself.

When you're aware you need another
    When you need the Lord, and a sis or a brother.
And sitting down to play dominoes
    Reminds you that life's highs and lows

Are best weathered with faith in God above
    And a few friends, some coffee and a little love.
And those are the times when it truly shows
    It's not really about the Dominoes.

Now I must confess I like to win.
    But my chances soon stretched very thin!

My son Micah began to slyly grin
    When it seemed apparent he would win.
Yes, the rest of us were soundly defeated.
    But he admitted after…doggone, he cheated.
The little rascal…can you believe
    He was stuffing dominoes up his sleeve!
Ruth never knew, I really don't think
    Although I wonder if I saw her wink…
But for weeks after that dominoes game
    She asked Micah to please come play again.
The thought often goes through my mind.
    Would he dare to cheat a second time?
Well, I doubt it matters, for everyone knows…
    It was never really about the Dominoes.

Note

    I shared this at Ruth's funeral. She had a double lung transplant a few years prior, and battled through many setbacks. She loved having a good time in the simplest of ways…like playing dominoes. And once, she dragged her oxygen tanks along onto an airplane with her on a trip to fulfil a lifelong dream of seeing Fogo, Twillingate and Morten's Harbour (Newfoundland), from the song "I'se the B'y." Even with all of her health challenges, her life reminds me to find joy in small and unexpected places.

My brother Tim, with his Canadian-made sports car, a 1975 Bricklin

Red Light!

I was cruising down the parkway late one night
When I pulled up to a red traffic light.
There beside me was a pedal-to-metal muscle machine.
His Maker had made him so strong, long and lean.
He rolled down the window and said "I can't be beat…
How 'bout we race to the end of the street?"
He said "I'm blessed with more zest under my hood…
I can go faster and long-laster than you ever could.

He was a bragger with more swagger than I'll ever know…
Did I dare to compare to this braggadocio?
He started squealing about feeling the need for more speed.
He got loud enough and proud enough to make eardrums bleed.
I just smiled and nodded as he poked and he prodded.
No part of him worked as hard as his jaw did!

As he yelled and bellowed and jested and joked.
And revved his engine as the air filled with smoke.
What a racket, what commotion, oh what a scene…
Then all of a sudden, the light turned to green.

He lunged forward with all of his might…
The tires all squealed out in sheerest delight.
With a big cloud of smoke, he roared out of sight,
As I gently lurched forward and calmly turned right.
The way he was headed was not my way at all.
For each of us follows our own unique call.

Though life is a race, it's not competition.
There is no need to jockey for position.
Following Christ is my one sole ambition.

That is my benchmark, that is my mission.
The need to be first must be diminished,
It only matters who gets to the finish.

Let me offer this one explanation:
Though mileage may vary, we share one destination.
If we go separate ways it might not be a mistake.
For there are different paths that we all might take.
As long as we're branches of the same vine,
You can go your way and I will go mine.
When it is finished, and this race has been won,
The Master will say to us each, well done.

Note

If you thought this one starts out sounding like "Dead Man's Curve" by Jan and Dean, you're right. As a preteen, I would sit in a corner of my older brother's bedroom and listen to vinyl albums of surf music, Elvis, then early Christian rock, and eventually Stryper. The *right turn* in this poem reminds us that we should not compare our own trajectory to the lives of others around us… God has a unique plan in mind for each of us.

A Healthy Team

Let me tell you a tale about being on teams…
Working together can be harder than it seems.
Unless it's a room full of mindless minions…
You can expect all kinds of differing opinions.
There once was a group of great minds debating,
An addition the local hospital was creating.
The project was huge and would cost lots of cash…
The dermatologist said, "I think this is rash."
The podiatrist was the next one to talk.
She said, "This is the path that we should walk."
The ear doctor said, "It is sound…so let's do it."
The radiologist said, "I can see right through it."
One doctor said the idea was spreading like fever.
The chaplain said he's tempted to be a believer.
The anaesthesiologist thought the idea was a gas.
The urologist said, "This too shall pass."
The ophthalmologist thought the architect was blind,
The psychiatrist couldn't make up his mind.
The obstetrician said, "It will take too much labour!"
And they started arguing, each with his neighbour.
The pediatrician said, "You're all acting like kids!"
And the brain surgeon said, "Have you all flipped your lids?"
It was doomed to failure, the writing's on the wall,
When the surgeon stood up and washed his hands of it all.
In the end, the project breathed its last breath;
The coroner said lack of agreement was cause of death.
The moral is simple: when it comes to unity,
You'll find that great minds don't always agree.

Hot Dog Church

Church is like a hot dog I hold in my hand…
But without the works, this church is too bland.
I'd still eat the hot dog, but I ask you this favour;
Put the works on this church and give it some flavour.

First start with red ketchup, it's a bold metaphor…
Of passionate people who keep shouting for more!
Then add the mustard in one long line of yellow.
Representing those are thoughtful and mellow.

Some just trust Jesus, they're never vexed or perplexed.
Those people are relish and it goes on next.
Some folk believe the church needs to be shaken!
They have their place in these crisp strips of bacon.

Some want to smell like the fragrance of Christ…
Hold your nose while these onions are chopped and diced!
When life gets spicy, some go all willy-nilly…
But God handles the hot stuff, so pour on the chili!

And then there are those who always remind us…
No matter what problems confound or confine us…
With confusion and friction and fighting at times…
Anxious moments when blood pressure climbs…

These folks remind you God's Church is a place…
Where each can find their own unique space…
These are the cheese that hold it together…
Reminding us all that we're in it forever.

The cheese melts all over like one sticky goo…

You're stuck with me…and I'm stuck with you.
Next time you have hot dogs, take this to heart…
Church is a place where we all take our part.

Maybe you're not relish, or ketchup or cheese…
Whatever you are, just be that thing, please.
When we all do that, just as we should…
God says, "I like it! This hot dog is good!"

Doormat

I'm sure you've had the odd day that
You feel like no more than a doormat
Those occasions when pesky people use
You, on which to wipe their shoes.
We're called to help, serve, love…and such
But sometimes people ask just too much.
Well, God knows where you live and toil
When you feel smudged with grime and soil.

But count it all joy, not sacrifice,
When what you've done, you've done for Christ.
And if others find the Lord, by stepping over me
Write "Welcome" on my forehead, for all the world to see.

I'd rather be a doormat into the house of God
Than to stand in the spotlight while the crowds applaud.
I'd rather be a doormat into the presence of the Lord
Than to be idolised and canonised, worshipped and adored.

No one likes that humble doormat feeling—
And being stepped on doesn't sound appealing!
If others stepped your way when passing through
Count it all joy that they came through you.
And when you reach heaven with your race run,
You'll hear Him say, "Come on in… Well done."
And others might not have made it, except…
You were the one on which they stepped.

Troy Tobey

Note

I shared this poem at my aunt Doreen's funeral as a tribute to her faithful service as a pastor's wife in small churches for sixty years. When my wife and I first started out in church work, Doreen once said, "We're just doormats for people to wipe their feet on." While that may not sound pleasant, it's a close parallel to Psalm 84:10, "I would rather be a doorkeeper in the house of my God." A true servant doesn't mind being the conduit by which people find God.

Finger-paints

Let me tell you a story, a sort of heavenly fable
Of a bunch of believers sitting down at a table.
They greet with a handshake, and a nervous smile
They all take their places and sit for a while.

No one seems to have too much to say
Till they all pull out finger-paints, and doodle away.
Every finger was painting, no matter their age,
Then one gal stood up and held up her page.

"Look at my drawing…it's a church with a steeple;
Inside I am preaching to 200 people."
She'd barely sat down, when another one stood,
And said, "Mine has 300…now isn't that good?"

Then one got up and cleared his throat,
"This is me, preaching out of a boat…
And all get converted, yes—the whole crowd.
"If God saw my picture, wouldn't He be proud?"

"Here in my painting," another man started,
"I'm reaching out to the broken-hearted.
That's me pulling them over heaven's bridge…
Do you think God would put this on His fridge?"

A lady then said, "I'm certain God's choice
Would be this picture of my angelic voice.
For as I am singing, 'How Great Thou Art'
Thousands ask Jesus to come into their heart."

Soon many were speaking, it was near a riot,
But a fellow named Bob sat there, all quiet.
His picture showed only himself and another.
He was sharing God's love with a prodigal brother.

Bob said to himself, "Well, mine isn't much…
No crowds or boats or steeples and such.
The others all painted a masterpiece.
It's easy to see that mine is the least."

Bob looked to the left, then looked to the right
In secret, he slid his art out of sight.
He crumpled it up into a ball
Then turned and threw it out into the hall.

Now, no one had noticed the Man near the door.
I can't say why they'd not seen Him before.
He said, "I've got something you all should see,
It's right this way, so come…follow Me."

He led them to a kitchen as big as the sun
And there was this fridge; it was second to none.
It seemed to be about three miles high
The top of it towered right to the sky.

They looked at the fridge, and were cut to the heart
It held row after row of finger-paint art.
All had their places; none seemed to stand out.
(I guess standing out is not what it's about.)

As they all turned to be on their way
I heard the kind Man good-heartedly say,
"Now, quit with your preening, and posing and jawing:
There's room on my fridge for everyone's drawing."

The kitchen emptied, except Bob and the Man.
Bob spied the page he'd crushed in his hand.
"I crumpled and crinkled it up in a ball…
So how come it seems to outshine them all?"

"It was My doing," the Man said, unabashed.
"Would I let a masterpiece go out with the trash?
"I smoothed it all out with a finishing touch…
What you thought was ugly, I loved so much!

When you finger-paint, I am just thrilled,
And an empty space on My fridge gets filled.
Just think 'I can,' and 'I am,' not 'I can't,' or 'I ain't."
And don't worry 'bout others…just paint, paint, paint!"

Note

    One of my favourite pieces I've ever done, "Finger-paints" was written as a tribute to Christian people everywhere who serve seemingly unnoticed. Someone notices. God sees what is done in secret (Matthew 6:4)!

Ketchup

If the ketchup was down to just one last drop…
Would you go buy another at the ketchup shop?
Or would you shake it and shake it and shake it non-stop
To get that last drop of ketchup to plop.

And what if life suddenly gave you the squeeze?
And not one single thing seemed to come with ease?
It just might be God bringing you to your knees…
Maybe that's why you're feeling the squeeze?

If you're going through one of those hard times
When you're shaken about like a bottle of Heinz
Remember that God works in ways of all kinds
And this just might be one of those times.

No, God isn't one to just cuddle and coddle
When shaking is needed, He's not one to dawdle!
With a shake and a jolt and a joggle full throttle
He'll get right down to the last of your bottle.

Be patient my friend, I must ask you, please
For this could be God giving you the squeeze
There's more to you than the average eye sees
But it never appears…until after the squeeze.

Life Lived in Caps

Some days life feels like a really hard go…
Winning or losing, you just don't know.
Some days you get the pot of gold, sometimes you get the scraps.
But either way, choose this day to live your life in CAPS.
Life to the full, that's what Jesus said.
So why do we live half-empty instead?
While we wait on God, maybe he waits on us perhaps…
To jump out and shout, I choose to live life in CAPS.
When your nerves are fried and your patience snaps
Just say, Lord help me today to live life in CAPS.
When life gives us hard slaps right across our yaps
We can choose even still to live life in CAPS.
When you're pulling yourself up by your own bootstraps
Give thanks for the strength to live life in CAPS.
On the days full of mischief, misdeeds and mishaps,
When we just can't go on and we want to collapse;
When life seems to be filled with its gaps and its traps…
Just remember the Lord promised us life lived in CAPS!
Don't live life halfway, don't live tentatively
Find your God-given purpose, and live bold and free.
If life is ho-hum, full of yawning and naps…
You'll one day regret not living life in CAPS.
Get up and get out there, and run a few more laps
Today's a fresh chance to live life in CAPS.
And when this life is all through and our days are all done.
And the Lord says, "Well done, my daughter, my son."
All of heaven is watching as we walk this sod…
And if you listen closely, you'll hear angels applaud.
The sound grows stronger as all heaven claps
It's for you that knew to live your life in CAPS.

Note

Not long before she died in 2016, Sheila had shared this phrase with me—*a life lived in caps.* I shared this tribute at her funeral as an encouragement that in spite of the tough road her life had been, she truly wanted to live life to the full, and to find God's best for her life.

My son, catching a wave on Lake Huron near our home

Surfer Psalm
(A Surfer's Paraphrase of Psalm 23)

Lord you are Boss; You give me all the rad waves I could ever carve.
(The Lord is my shepherd; I shall not want.)
You make me tuck into gnarly barrels;
(He leads me beside still waters. He restores my soul.)
You take the drop through calm channels. You chill me to hang loose when I'm totally noodled.
(He makes me lie down in green pastures.)
You show me how to curl through bommie waves and I am totally aggro about your label.
(He leads me in paths of righteousness for his name's sake.)
Even when I go backside through the churley in the steep of the boneyard, it's all copacetic, bruh…
(Even though I walk through the valley of the shadow of death, I will fear no evil.)
You got my back.
(For you are with me.)
Your fin and your leash leave me totally rad chill.
(Your rod and your staff, they comfort me.)
You goat boat me through a paddle battle with barneys, jakes and grey suits.
(You prepare a table before me in the presence of my enemies.)
You deck me out in tubular merch, and my quiver is full of awesome shortboards, skegs and twinfins.
(You anoint my head with oil; my cup overflows.)
No jokes, You send me down the line into epic conditions at dawn each day,
(Surely goodness and mercy shall follow me all the days of my life.)
…And I will totally carve in the glass house of the Big Kahuna in endless summer. Cowabunga!
(And I shall dwell in the house of the Lord forever.)

Our church overlooks Lake Huron. Sometimes sunsets are visible in the reflection.

Compelling Church

There once was three fellas who set out on a search;
To find what makes for a really good church.
They walked all day, all over town…
Then met to discuss what each one had found.
The first one said, the church I like best…
Is extremely large and elaborately blest.
They have stained glass windows and big wooden doors
And long comfy pews and shiny clean floors.
The budget is healthy and the bills are all paid.
Now this is a church that has got it made!
This church was so perfect, this church was so nice;
I took some photos and walked past it twice.
I saw the reverend and said, "Can I come in?"
He said, "Oh heavens, no; we've just got it clean!
It's been all spruced for our Sunday crowd.
Let you walk in? well, its just not allowed."
The next spoke up and said I've found the one:
A church filled with laughter, bursting with fun.
They have lots of programs, they'll keep you real busy…
If you signed up for it all you would get quite dizzy!

There's study groups, checkers and basketball courts…
Art classes, music and all kinds of sports.
It's hip and its modern, and up with the trends.
But no one saw me, and I didn't make friends.
Everyone was so busy all running about…
I softly walked in, and unnoticed walked out.
Then the last one spoke and said, "I've found the place.
Where people show love and kindness and grace.
They saw me coming and they came out to greet me
And someone said they were so glad to meet me.

You'll get a big hug unless you say no…
But if you let them hug you, they will not let go.
They smile with a smile that says God truly loves you…
And I couldn't help thinking that they loved me too.
They sat me down and they just let me talk.
They didn't care what chair and didn't watch the clock.
I talked about my job and my kids and my wife.
And they said God has a wonderful plan for my life.
I felt such a peace beyond all explanation.
Now that church my friends, is a soul-saving station."
The three friends just sat there until one replied,
What makes a great church is the people inside.
It's not programs or budgets or whistling and belling…
It's love, grace and mercy that makes church compelling.

Go and Do Likewise

It should come as no surprise…
The enemy comes in a disguise.
He tries to pull wool over your eyes;
To scrutinise, scandalise and vandalise.
To despise and disenfranchise.
With lies he tries to jeopardise…
To paralyse and sterilise…
But let the church of Christ arise!

If only we would realise…
The enemy cannot contain you guys!
The Word of God testifies.
Noah believed before he saw the waters rise.
Abraham trusted what he could not see with his eyes… Go and do likewise.
Hannah prayed, and the Lord heard her cries…
Joshua took the land with no compromise… Go and do likewise!
Caleb believed in spite of ten pessimistic spies.
By faith David cut a giant down to size… Go and do likewise.
Mary offered herself to God's salvific enterprise
Twelve men left all to become the Nazarene's allies… Go and do likewise.
The early church stood faithful through both lows and highs…
Paul endured the suffering ever with his eyes on the prize… Go and do likewise!
Let the church of Christ arise!
Unto Jesus, turn your eyes…
For grace and strength He multiplies!
We've been sent out to evangelise,
We've been mobilised to globalise…
To teach and preach and to baptise.
Let all vocalise the devils' demise.
For the Spirit comes to authorise and energise…
That we might go and do likewise!

THE SONG

We shared one last conversation, not too long before he died.
There were hugs and handholding (but no tears were cried).
Talk of life and love, of family and the Lord,
But I'll tell you when our chat really struck a chord…
I asked about his many years spent in Christian ministry;
Of all the times and places, his favourite memory?
He didn't take too long, he answered right away.
"The songs. Yes, the songs," that's what he had to say.

He would be busy working when the groups began to sing,
And he'd listen as joyous jubilation began to ring.
I could see his gleaming eyes, I know that he just beamed
Every time he heard praises sung, the song of the redeemed.
Many cultures and ethnicities, but unified in song.
And knowing John, I'll bet he did his best to sing along.
I must say how it touched my heart that he would answer thus…
Reminds me again that serving God is not just about us.

With all our talents and our efforts, we will come and go.
Him Who is, and was and is to come…is the true Star of this show.
But as much as John loved that music, as good as it could get
I'm telling you, my friend, he hadn't heard nothing yet.
For as he left this earth, to be present with the Lord
I'd guess that the sound of heaven left him absolutely floored.
To see Jesus in the center, being worshipped and adored.
While ten thousand times ten thousand gloriously roared.

Every tribe, every nation, every people, every tongue.
Serenading Jesus with the sweetest song ever sung.
Can't you picture it, as this throng sings the song
With tears down his cheeks, as John joins in to sing along.

We will miss him greatly, now that he is gone.
We may feel that something's missing, as life is moving on.
As we say farewell for now, to the dearly departed…
For John the song has just begun, and the party's only started.

Note

This was a tribute I shared at my uncle John's funeral. He served in Christian ministry his whole life until he died in his eighties: as a pastor, principal in a Christian school, dean in a Christian college… But when I asked about his most endearing memory of ministry, he said it was when he and his wife (my aunt Ann) ran a Christian campground and they would listen to the vibrant praise music of groups renting the facility. He loved to listen to them worshipping God, often in their own language or cultural expression…a precursor to heaven no doubt!

Not about Jane

I am under strict orders, she made it quite plain.
I'm here to talk about Jesus, and not about Jane.
Don't get me wrong; please let me explain…
And please don't think that I mean to complain.
See, I'd love to tell you about our very first meeting.
It was a simple handshake and a kindly greeting.
But I shan't waste your time on things so mundane;
I'm here to talk about Jesus, not about Jane.
I would go for a visit, to talk family and such,
And weather and travel, and the odd word in Dutch.
But the topic was testimony again and again…
She wanted to talk about Jesus, and not about Jane.

"Wonderful, Counselor, Mighty God, Prince of Peace,
Saviour, Redeemer, Whose wonders never cease;
Jesus—the name that breaks every chain…
He deserves all the glory," so testifies Jane.
Humbly, sincerely, and not afraid to confess…
"My life without Jesus? I'd be a mess!"
You'd hear about Jesus, if you picked her brain…
You'll end up talking about Jesus, when you talk to Jane.
Today there is time to cry, to sing and to pray.
Welcome one and all, to Jane's Graduation Day.
The Word says, "To live is Christ, to die is gain."
Jesus has been waiting to welcome dear Jane.
That's the gospel story…a life that is changed.
And Heaven awaits us…it's all been arranged.
I hope I've made plain, something so simple, so true
What Jesus did for Jane, He can also do for you.

Note

When Jane became ill and she had an inkling that her time on earth was short, she made this statement a number of times in reference to her funeral: "It's not about me." She truly wanted her life to reflect her faithful service to Jesus Christ.

An Unfinished Quilt

When I think about this life that I have built
I realise I am an unfinished quilt.
Piece by piece I've tried to create
Something that is magnificently great.
But some stitching is missing, and some pieces don't match.
The border's disordered and it needs the odd patch.
I dreamt of a tapestry, designed to the hilt…
But I ended up with an unfinished quilt.
Some lines are crooked and some spots are rough.
Maybe I just was not quite good enough?
And just when I'm feeling the stirring of guilt,
I hear the Lord say, "I quite like your quilt.
In my grace you have toiled and your work is now done
It's just as I wanted, dear daughter, dear son.
So don't cry and don't fret, as if milk has been spilt.
Leave it with me, your unfinished quilt.
You blazed a trail, you did your part…
And where you left off, others will start.
They'll add their own colours, and fabrics as well.
And where it ends up, who can possibly tell?
For you now, the pains and labours have ceased
So enter your rest in joy and in peace."

As for us…we may have questions and doubts.
Wondering how life will ever work out…
But have faith and trust God when life gets all tilted.
To God be the glory for the lives we have quilted.

Note

Julie was very quiet about her life, her service to others, and the illness that eventually took her life. When she passed at a fairly young age, she left an unfinished quilt. I shared this tribute at her funeral, drawing the parallel to life. We are all—in so many ways—unfinished quilts. Keep working on me, Lord!

Party in the Barn

I came to Bethlehem one night, following a star.
I'd walked for such a long time, following from afar.
I went to the innkeeper as soon as I was able.
I asked about the party; he said it's in the stable.
The party's in the stable? How could this be?
That didn't sound like much of a party to me!
"You surely must be joking, spinning me a yarn…
How could such a special party be held in a barn?"
But I walked out to the stable to sneak a little peep
There were cows and lambs and goats, and a handful of sheep.
A grumpy donkey stood in the corner, tall and slim.
I doubt if anyone would dare to pin a tail on him!
There was no birthday singing, no happy juggling clown:
Just a bunch of poor shepherds, quietly kneeling down.
No pile of presents wrapped with ribbons and with bows
The only gift was in the manger, wrapped in swaddling clothes.
Meek, mild and humble, one precious birthday Boy;
Jesus came to give us the gift of everlasting joy!

And They're Off!

"And they're off," says the announcer, what a glorious sound!
And away we all go, around and around.
I think in a way life is like one long horse race.
Bigger than Flamboro or Woodbine or any other place!
On the racetrack of life many battles are fought;
Sometimes you crawl, and some days you trot.
Some will do anything to get to first place.
But some things matter more than winning the race.
Oh, we all want the trophies and cups and ribbons of course,
But let's not let the cart get ahead of the horse…
When it gets in your blood you need not be coerced…
You'd still love to be racing whether in first or the worst.
And life can be like that, on so many days.
You're galloping along, when things go sideways.
You get dirt in your teeth and dust in your eyes.
But keep your hands on the reins and your eyes on the prize.
No matter what place you finally finish
The joy of the journey cannot be diminished.
When we cross the line and our race is all done
Who will recall all the ribbons we've won?
At the end of it all, when push comes to shove.
The trophies that count are the people you love.

Note

I shared this tribute at my uncle Dennis' funeral. He was in harness racing for many years, and that topic provided a great metaphor for priorities in life. Dennis was dearly loved and respected by many family and friends.

Lord, let my life shine for you!

Neon

This little light of mine? Nope. I won't sing that line. I want to be a big light that shines bright. I am not a match that is lit only for a minute. Or a candle in the window, flickering as the winds blow. And I'm not a lighter, shining only long enough to light something else up. No. I am a shiner. I am a burner. I always want to be on; I wanna shine like neon.

I never want to burn up, sizzle out, or flame down. I want to light up the night, to dispel the darkness. I was born to be bright, and I live to be luminescent. Not a soft phosphorescence or a faint, flickering flame. I am not a flash in the pan. I am a floodlight on the darkest night, dispelling doom and gloom. From dusk till dawn, I wanna shine like neon.

Kings and queens may tumble, empires may crumble. The world may come undone, and evil thinks it's won. But when darkness rears its ugly head, all the more light must be shed. Brightness is rightness, and the shadows can go back under the rock they crawled out from under.

Isn't this something we can agree on? Don't we all wanna shine like neon?

Though tables turn and stomachs churn while dreamers yearn, I must burn. God would have me grow so that my light will glow; I've been ransomed and redeemed, so I can radiate with brilliancy and resiliency… Why would I settle for a twinkle or a spark? That will not push back the dark. Sorry for this rant that I must be on… but I must shine like neon.

I won't settle for glistening and gleaming, for I was born for beaming. I've been put here for such a time as this. I am a headlight, a high beam. I want to be a garish glare that makes others stop and stare… Stare at the Saviour…look to the Lord. Gaze at His greatness. View the victorious One. In shining, we show the way to Christ; He who for us was sacrificed. If only my little light might have some small part in pushing back the dark. My job has been done when others see the Son. Is this the path you wish to be on? Then join me and shine like neon.

OL' MR. JONES

Bobby's family moved next door
To 27 Sycamore,
The home of mean ol' Mr. Jones.

And who do you think was up at dawn,
Keeping watch on his front lawn?
Yes, it was mean ol' Mr. Jones.

Mr. Jones was rude and crass;
When anyone dared step on his grass!
But no one told Bobby about mean ol' Mr. Jones.

Once Bobby went to fetch a ball;
He shouldn't have gone over there at all…
On the lawn of mean ol' Mr. Jones.

Mr. Jones gave Bobby's mom a note;
"Stay off my lawn" was all he wrote
Bobby's mom said, "Don't go on the lawn of Mr. Jones."

One day Bobby rode his bicycle upon;
The front left corner of Mr. Jones's lawn
And out came mean ol' Mr. Jones.

"Stay off my lawn, you mangy kid!
Look at all the harm you did!"
He'd flipped his lid, mean ol' Mr. Jones.

"I'm sorry sir, I never meant…
To cause such an accident!"
But the door swung shut behind mean ol' Mr. Jones.

A sign went up; it simply said…
"Trespassers will be shot dead!
Sincerely, Mr. Jones."

Now Bobby's old enough to read it;
And he's surely smart enough to heed it,
But he went and tried to seed it…the lawn of mean ol' Mr. Jones.

He got right down into the soil;
And planted grass seed with great toil
Fixing the lawn of mean ol' Mr. Jones.

Through the door the neighbour burst…
"Get out of here, you've made it worse!"
He began to curse and curse…that mean ol' Mr. Jones!

It didn't look too good that day;
Didn't seem that love would find a way
With the mean ol' heart inside mean ol' Mr. Jones.

But Bobby knew just what to do;
He broke his piggy bank in two
And took off with his little wagon…past the lawn of mean ol' Mr. Jones.

He went down to the hardware store;
And filled the wagon three times or more
It wasn't going to be easy to love mean ol' Mr. Jones.

He waited until that very night;
And there by just the moon's dim light
Bobby worked on the lawn of mean ol' Mr. Jones.

The next day, Mr. Jones thought it odd
His lawn was covered with fresh sod
And a scribbled note said, "Sorry, Mr. Jones."

"What in the world…?" was all he said,
As Mr. Jones just scratched his head.
He was speechless, that mean ol' Mr. Jones.

Bobby knows how green grass grows
So for days and days he ran a hose
Through the fence, to water the lawn of mean ol' Mr. Jones.

Bobby's parents had been watching as well
And they were smart enough to tell
Bobby was getting through to mean ol' Mr. Jones.

Not long after, Mr. Jones took sick
And his front lawn grew long and thick
But Bobby cut the grass for mean ol' Mr. Jones.

It was about five years or more
That Bobby cut the grass next door.
And he became friends with mean ol' Mr. Jones.

Bobby's not a boy no more;
He's got a family and he runs a store.
But he still shows love to mean ol' Mr. Jones.

Do you think love can find a way?
Can love break through and win the day
With a mean ol' heart like mean ol' Mr. Jones?

Now once a week, on his own hours
Bobby cuts the grass and plants some flowers
At the grave of his friend, Mr. Jones.

Note

Neighbours are such a blessing. They often bless us with kind words, friendly gestures, and opportunities to develop character! This poem was inspired by a next-door neighbour we had when our kids were babies, who complained that the whine from our air conditioner was keeping him awake at night. I tried to run it through the day and turn it off at night, but the next day a colossal heatwave rolled into town! I think we blest those neighbours most when we moved away a few months later!

Whatever the weather, keep your eyes upon the Son.

Look to the Son

Some would whine for only sunshine
If they could have their way…
Blue skies and record highs
Each and every day.

There'd be no rain; there'd be no pain,
Just frolicking in the sun.
There'd be no heat, there'd be no sleet
Just pleasant sunny fun.

This warming trend would never end
Picnic-perfect weather.
Rain or snow? I'll tell you friend…
The best time would be never!

But life's not like that, truth be told
Not like that at all…
Spring is wet, winter cold,
And it's too chilly in the fall!

The highs and lows, they comes and goes
Winds of change are never done.
Hurricanes and tornadoes
Threaten to block out the Son.

Beyond prediction or description
Life burns and it also freezes.
Both hot and cold, winds brash and bold
But rarely gentle breezes!

Though winds clatter, it is no matter
I pay it no never mind.
Stormy or fair I don't really care
I'm not the fair-weather kind.

I'll follow the Lord though rain be outpoured
Or hailstorms have begun.
Neither snow nor sleet give me cold feet
I've got my eyes upon the Son.

Let winds blow, and storm clouds grow
Bring on the precipitation…
No aftershock can break this rock
I'm on a sure foundation!

When weather's inclement, fear's always present
And others may take and run.
But with face to the wind, somewhat thick-skinned
I look up to see the Son.

Others may shy as heatwaves fry
And some shrivel in the frost
But I'm not scared… I came prepared
I knew to count the cost!

I've been clothed and shod by the grace of God
With double stitching on all my patches.
Do your worst, stormy burst!
I've battened down my hatches.

Typhoons and monsoons, by light of the moon,
This test shall soon be won.
When the wind is all blown and I'm chilled to the bone
I'll soon be warmed by the Son.

Go ahead and wail, you stormy gale,
I shall not come undone.
Whatever the weather I shall forever
Keep my eyes upon the Son.

Cream Puff!

You can learn so much about life with one quick stop
At your local neighbourhood doughnut shop.

Look through the glass and you soon realise
That life, like doughnuts, comes in every shape and size.

Some grab for the biggest, like a giant apple fritter…
But before you reach the end, you find it just tastes bitter.

Some want super sweet, Boston cream they demand!
But less gets in your mouth, than what's left on your hand!

Some would say the cruller is a doughnut beyond compare…
But when you bite inside, you find it's mostly air!

What's the best of all these doughnuts, pound for pound and ounce for ounce?
Well, that's simple! It's the cream puff, because it's what's inside that counts.

Someone said to eye the size of doughnut, not the size of the hole…
Don't be counting money, toys and friends while forgetting about your soul!

Some will swoon for sprinkles, or go gaga for some glazing…
But when God works deep inside us, it truly is amazing!

Don't focus on the fanciest, don't give in to your pride.
It's not the outer shell that counts, it's the stuff inside.

When it comes to what's best for us, we may not even know.
But He's the Master Baker; we are just the dough.

You and I are cream puffs, when our very sweetest part
Is the thick and rich deposit God has placed within the heart.

Note

    This was a tribute to Fred, who had doughnut baker on his resume! Just before he died, I asked him his favourite type of doughnut, and when he said cream puff, it made me think of the creamy filling as a metaphor for what truly matters in life.

The walls at Louisbourg, a French fortress
built in Nova Scotia in the 1700s

Walls

What if there were walls around us like a wall around a city,
Walls that kept us from our destiny, wouldn't that be a pity?
Walls around our hearts, and walls around our lives;
Walls around our children, and walls around our wives.
Walls to hem us in, and walls to keep us out.
Walls of fear and failure, discouragement and doubt.
Walls so high they reach the sky and near block out the sun;
Walls that taunt and haunt us…this battle can't be won.
Walls that say, "No farther! You shall never pass!"
Walls of stone and granite, walls of iron and brass.
And what if God said, "These walls will fall, if you follow what I say."
Would you be willing to ditch it all, to simply just obey?
It doesn't take a majority, you don't need a committee…
God seeks for one obedient son, who wants to take the city.
Can I take God at His word, I really have to wonder…
Or would I grab a shovel and try to tunnel under?
Would I grab a pickaxe and try to break on through?
Or could I step back, and watch what God would do?
He says "March around it, and let me do the rest"
Will you just be obedient, or will you now protest?
I think I'd lace up running shoes, and start marching around
I'd march until my steps had worn a path upon the ground.
I'd march two times, three and four, whatever it may take
Five or six or seven more, until those big walls shake.
I feel for the one who quits too soon, it is such a pity…
That he will never see the Lord giving Him the city.
Keep faith, my friends, believe and just stay humble.
God has promised us the city, these walls are going to crumble.
March on through wind and rain, through all the nitty-gritty…
The time is coming closer now, when the Lord gives us the city!
All I'm saying is don't stop praying and marching all around

The time is near when we will hear that glorious trumpet sound…
Destiny waits beyond the gates, and it might not be pretty
But let it out, give a shout, as the Lord gives us the city!

Note

This poem was part of a sermon on Gideon and the walls of Jericho (Joshua 6), a reminder that we can't give up…keep on believin'!

The Veil

Lord, You have made me, I know this to be true.
Made with the purpose of drawing closer to You.
But my sin and guilt were fetters that I could not break through.
I wanted to know You better, but what was I to do?
Your holiness and glory I could not even view
For my shameful, sinful story I could not undo.
Sin's not just annoying, like a pebble in a shoe…
It's more like the boring of a giant hole in a canoe!
When I tried to fight it, I found it only grew.
Iniquity left a mark on me, one giant sin tattoo
And as the temple had a veil of purple, red and blue,
There was an airtight curtain, keeping me from You.
In and of myself, I would not have had a clue
As to how I could ever get any closer to You.
All my striving and my stretching, the best that I could do
Wasn't doing anything to break the veil in two.
I was destined to be destitute, and far away from You.
But amazingly You did for me what only You could do…
In Your grace, You took my place, You've gloriously broken through
Top to bottom it was awesome when you tore the veil in two.
The veil is torn, I've been reborn, I'm alive and I'm brand new!
Now I can see a glimpse of glory since You tore the veil in two.
Roses are red, they say, and violets are blue…
Grace has won, the veil is gone, all because of You.
This tattered veil could not prevail to keep me from You!
Praise Your name again and again, You tore the veil in two!

A Very Fine Coat

When the storm kicks up and cold wind blows…
I brace myself and bury my nose
Into the warmth of this very fine coat.
I'm so glad I'm perfectly dressed…
For winter's most furious test
Thank the Lord for this very fine coat.
It's red and blue and white and green…
And sharp and stark and long and lean
I wonder have you ever seen such a glorious coat?
But wait just a minute, I cannot deny it…
I didn't make it, and I didn't buy it.
Someone gave me this very fine coat.
I used to have others that I had fashioned…
Some of them zipped up and some of them fastened
But none were as good as this very fine coat.

Some were quite ugly, some were quite proud…
Some were quite haughty, or gaudy and loud
Some were too big and some were too small…
None did me justice, no, none at all.
Some weighed me down so I could not run…
And some wrinkled and shriveled with the hot summer sun.
I tried real hard but to my chagrin…
None of those coats could cover my sin…
Though I shrouded myself as best as I could…
None of my efforts did any good.
All my inadequacies came right through…
The apparel I'd chosen just wouldn't do.
But along came Jesus, someone cue the choir…
For He decked me out in all new attire.
Though I had been a low-down dirty varmint…

He dressed me in a heavenly garment.
A righteous robe, and salvation apparel…
Not bad for a guy caught over a barrel!
My very best had been filthy rags only…
I'd been a loser, a louse and a phoney…
But Jesus gave me this very fine coat.
And someday when I'm standing in glory…
And each of us tells our very own story,
I will want to talk about this very fine coat.
I know that day will come for me…
This coat is my guarantee.
This is a coat of inheritance.
It's a very glorious coat. It's most victorious coat.
It's a coat of royalty. It's a coat made just for me.
This coat is one of a kind. This coat gives me peace of mind.
Sling your arrows through the air. I'm protected in this coat's care.
This coat gives me identity. I'm a child of the King and I am free.
Its second to none, and blest by the One
Who gave Himself for me.
Here me now, all you folks…
All my other coats, suits and cloaks
I've traded them for this one here.
I've traded my sins and my faults and my fear.

It's lightweight, it's strong, and it's fireproof…
If you had to buy it you'd go through the roof!
It's oh so costly, but He gave it for free…
It can do for you what it did for me…
There's only one place this coat can be gotten…
If you're good or you're bad or you're downright rotten…
Just ask Jesus… He has a very fine coat for you.

Through the Roof

If you're lying in the street and you cannot stand
I'd say you're in need of a good helping hand.

A few friends would be good, to help you around
In case Jesus the Healer comes to your town.

A few friends could carry you right to the place
So you could see Jesus, up close, face to face.

Just don't pick a friend who looks in through the door
And says, "Too bad for you, there's room for no more!"

And would a true friend peek in on the crowd
And say, "Jesus is there…but you're not allowed?"

No… If you've picked a good friend, a passionate one
He will not give up till the job is done.

"It just can't be done…" is that what friends say?
Or do they stand up and shout, "There must be a way!"

Do they rally the troops and pick up that bed?
Or do they just walk away and leave you for dead?

Are they good friends? Here's undeniable proof…
If they carry you up and let you down through the roof.

If they heave and they ho and pass you down from above
I'd say that's faith. It's gutsy. It's love.

If it were me on that mat, I'll tell you the truth…
I'd want a friend who'll take me up on the roof.

And Jesus had touched me and gave me my healing
I'd shout out my 'thank yous' with passion and feeling!

Don't think me haughty or proud or aloof…
I'm just trying to be someone who goes through the roof.

This Is A Book

This is a book. Look at this book.
Search high and low, by hook or by crook…
You'll not find an equal to this book.
Though ground give way and the earth be shook…
Still will stand this glorious book.
If you need a wise word or two…
I'm sure this book would surely do.
There's life and love, and hope inside…
And the cure for self, and sin and pride.
How many fires has it ignited?
How many times each hour recited?
Shouted and spouted from countless lips…
Saving souls and launching ships.
It's not just a book of laws and rules.
It's not just for fiends and fools.
It's a book of wisdom tried and true…
It's God's book and it's for you.
Are you looking for this kind of book?
That offers hope to the incurable crook?
If you're seeking love in a hopeless place…
This is a book that offers grace.
When all that can be taken has already been took,
And there seems no way to get off the hook
You can find the Lord in this amazing book.
When you're falling fast, it's your grappling hook.
When you've lost your way, it's a shepherd's crook.
It's a light to steer you through all the gobbledygook…
I have no fear of the donnybrook…
Thank the Lord for His awesome book!
When evil seems to run amok…
And someone has just took your rook

And if it seems your goose is cooked…
And you don't know where else to look…
Though enemies sneer and fists are shook;
Take the stance that I have took…
And stand firm upon this glorious book!

Troy Tobey

My Favourite Things

Raindrops of mercy and showers of blessing
Forgiveness of sinners most humbly confessing
Great faith and hope that salvation brings…
These are a few of my favourite things!

Fellowship, family and friends in high places.
The favour of God and all of His good graces.
Strength to soar as on eagles' wings
These are a few of my favourite things.

When the waves crash
When the wind stings
When life overpowers me…
I simply remember my favourite things
And I feel like royalty.

Dressed like a bride without spot or wrinkle
Blessed till my eyes have a permanent twinkle.
Filled with a hope that eternally springs
These are a few of my favourite things.

Joy beyond measure and love everlasting.
Endued with power through prayer and fasting
Destined to access the riches of kings
These are a few of my favourite things!

When my bones ache
When my heart breaks
When I'm feeling blue
I simply remember my favourite things
And Lord, I give thanks to You!

Note

A tribute to the classic song from *The Sound of Music*. Or maybe you guessed that already.

At a Time Like This

I know you can worship when life is swell,
And everything is going well
And you're living in a joyous bliss…
But it must be explored…
Can you still praise the Lord…AT A TIME LIKE THIS?

Do you still have a joyful song
When everything has gone wrong
And your life is one big swing and a miss…
Now please don't ignore me,
But can you give God all the glory…AT A TIME LIKE THIS?

When evil seems to have the day
And it seems a struggle to kneel and pray,
When you can almost hear the sound of a wicked hiss…
Does it sound odd
To say that God is still God AT A TIME LIKE THIS?

When you feel confused, upset or afraid;
When you feel used, alone or betrayed;
And your dearest friend walks up with a Judas kiss—
Does it even occur to you
That God is faithful and true…AT A TIME LIKE THIS?

Life is not always a bed of red roses,
And there may be days when every door closes…
But make the choice to raise your voice when life has got you in fits…
Give it all that you've got,
Give Him praise as you ought…AT A TIME LIKE THIS!

One of our Team Sunday photos at Lakeshore, 2019

Tag Team

So you think that's that? You gonna pin me to the mat? You're thinking that I'm down and out? Going down for the count…well, before you start dancing around, I'm just gonna warn ya, take a look in my corner…

See, I'm part of a tag team. And maybe you got the best of me… I confess you've made a mess of me…and maybe you've done it breathlessly… But I'm tagging my partner just now and pow… here he comes, over the ropes, and suddenly, I got high hopes. Because He's undefeated and always in His prime. Never been unseated, down through all of time. And I got a hunch that His one-two punch is enough to turn the tide. So glad I'm on His side! When He tips the scales, the gates of hell cannot prevail. Because He never ever fails, so I'll gladly ride His coat-tails…

The tale of the tape says He is in impeccable shape… Uncontainable. Unrestrainable. Indefatigable. Unparalleled and invulnerable. He is the ultimate prize fighter. He is a revival fire igniter. He is a miracle provider. He is the X-factor. He is the original power reactor. A human life impactor. I was about to take the fall, but here comes the undisputed heavyweight champion of it all… He is the Lord of lords and the King of kings, and here He comes to take my place in the ring… You can try to avoid Him, but He'll keep knockin' at your door. Try to wear Him down, but He keeps coming back for more. For those who are sinking, He's the shoreline. For the lost, He is the road sign. To the poor, He's a gold mine. To the thirsty. To the dull and dreary, He's the bright shine. To the weak and weary, He is the lifeline.

He has been orchestrating comebacks, smackdowns, and breakthroughs since before time began… He is the One, the Only, He is the Man… His name is Jesus!

Note

For the past few years in our church, we've used a sports metaphor in our sermon on Super Bowl Sunday (first Sunday in February). The Bible mentions "running the race" and training as a boxer, and sports images often project a powerful perspective on the Christian life... Plus, I love sports!

BAGGAGE

Most of us carry at least some baggage around;
Some of us look like a whole lost and found!
I will admit I've got my own bag or two…
Hey, life happens…what can you do?
I've got a suitcase as full as can be
With all the things others said about me.
One case is full of frustrations and fears
I've been adding to it for many long years.
One is full of the dreams that I wanted for me
The one marked "top secret" has a big lock and key.
There's one marked shame, and another called blame
And some of my suitcases don't even have a name.
There's a label marked losses and a carton marked "cautious"
And a box full of my self-inflicted crosses.
There's cartons and jars and an old burlap sack
And old wooden crates, piled up stack after stack.
There's batches of boxes crammed full of junk
And all of it piled on top of a huge trunk.
My baggage defines who I was and will be
My baggage outlines what it means to be me.
My baggage goes with me, wherever I go
I do still get there, but I have to go slow.
One day I stepped up to the train station wicket
And asked how much it would cost for one ticket.
The attendant smiled big and announced happily
"Your ticket's been paid for, so take it, it's free."
I was vexed and perplexed, how could this be?
Who would have purchased this ticket for me?
I gathered my things and then turned to go
But a voice stopped me cold with a sharp "No, no, no!"

It was the conductor… He would not let me through
He said "You can't bring all that stuff with you."
"One carry-on is all you can bring."
"You must choose only one single thing."
I thought, "No way… I cannot decide…
Which is the one to bring on the ride?"
I'll never survive without all the rest…
I'll never decide which one is best!
Should I bring dreams, and my great expectations?
Should I bring my pride and my indignations?
My fears and my tears, my faith and my doubt
These are things that I can't live without.
And I cannot leave the opinions of others,
Of father and mother, and sister and brothers.
Who would I be without all the debris
Of everything everyone ever said about me?
My eyes teared up and I sat down right there
As I fussed and I stressed and threw my hands in the air.
I was about to give up and just walk away
When the kind conductor stepped forward to say,
"I think there's a bag here that is just the one
The one suitcase that will get it done."
He retrieved one little bag, nothing more…
I'd never seen that bag before.
The bag was quite heavy, it was shiny and new…
It said, "All of the things God thinks about you."
The bag fell open and its treasures spilled out…
It boggled the mind and shattered all doubt.
God thinks I'm special, I am one of a kind.
I am unique, I am a rare find.
I am royal, I'm chosen, I am redeemed…
I am destined for more than I ever dreamed.
Others may speak disparagingly…
I've seen what God thinks about me.

They can mock me and shock me and speak adversely
I don't care… I know what God thinks of me.
All of the baggage in all of the earth
Cannot contain what I am or what I'm worth…
Who I was, who I am and who I will be
Can only be found in what God thinks of me.

Super Ball

Lord, I want to be a super ball…
To rise every time I fall.
That even when I drop from height,
Everything will be all right.

I know I may feel like a yo-yo…
So could we maybe start slow?
I want to be able to bounce with every ounce of my being.
But sometimes I'm seeing only the downsides and downslides of life…
It's hard as you plummet
To think of reaching the summit.
And sometimes I'm finding that I need reminding
That you've got a plan for this super ball man…
Lord send me some hope like a pulley and rope or a springboard, anything Lord.
A ladder would help when I can't do it myself.
When Life gets me down and I feel like the ground just won't let me go,
And I know the times when gravity has an awful pull on me.
But I was made for a trajectory that takes me from here to eternity.
Though I may hit the floor with a smack, believe you me, I will bounce back…
God made me to soar, not to languish on the floor.
I just want to bounce, that's all, like a super ball.
To bounce up when I've taken another fall,
And to remember what this is all about.
That down is not out.
That down is not done for.
That I can rise once more.
I'll reach for the ladder.

I know there will be one. Even if I don't see one.
There's a rising again for me,
I know there must be…
Right here and now maybe I can't tell you how…
But I can tell you why, this super ball was made to fly!

Pirate on Board

My boat's cargo hold is filled with treasures untold…
More precious than rubies, worth more than gold.
All this time, dutifully we have labored out on the open sea
With wind at our backs, we make our way speedily.
I'm serving my Lord, I'm serving the crown…
And nothing no nothing can slow this boat down.
There's a destination waiting up ahead…
Straight as an arrow, onwards we sped.
But then comes the word, from among the crew…
Without warning and right out of the blue…
Fit to be tied, flabbergasted and floored…
There's rumours afoot of a pirate on board!
This cannot be, I shout right out loud…
I pause for a prayer with my own head bowed…
Dear God there is one, who would your plans thwart…
Lord help us find and bind this mischievous sort.
He won't have this ship, I will not allow it!
I will nab him, I'll grab him; I decree and I vow it.
We'll search every cabin, and swab clean every deck…
Every hatch shall be opened, all the rigging be checked.

Then comes the word, the culprit's been found.
Come on, sailors, gather around.
Throw him in the brig, as big iron doors clank…
Or better yet, we'll make him walk the plank.
We can't have a traitor aboard this fine ship….
For sooner or later, he'll ruin this trip.
Who is this rascal that defies the Lord's plan…
I want to look in the eyes of this forsaken man.
Down the stairs, through the hall, Into cabin #3…
I burst through the door, but how can this be?

I look in the mirror, and go weak in the knee…
The pirate in question is in fact, me.
I am the one who too many times…
Defies my Lord, for my own designs.
Far too often I still disobey…
I grab the wheel and turn it my way.
In spite of my very best of intention,
It happens more times than I care to mention.
I know to go left but still I turn right.
I know to surrender, but still I will fight.
I know to drop anchor, but still I speed on…
I hope no one sees in the dark before dawn.
Lord, help me to be free of this piracy I see in me.
From sea to shining sea,
May Your grace and mercy be seen in me.
My Captain and Commander, take this old man from me,
And cast his self-centred heart into the depths of the sea.
No pirates allowed. No buccaneers neither…
We've no time for scallywags or mutinous deceivers.
I give you my whole heart, from crow's nest to keel,
Captain and commander, come take the wheel.

On highways and byways, the Shepherd seeks the lost.

SOS

What is an SOS?
SOS is sounding the alarm.
SOS is saving from harm.
But beware, for it is unsafe and unsound.
It's going out when dangers abound.
SOS is the shepherd leaving the fold,
When the chills of the cold multiply winds blowing bold.
SOS is seeking out souls over hill, over dale.
Through darkest of night, and the sleet and the hail.
You cannot stay home shouting, 'SOS, SOS!'
You must risk it all, you can do no less.
You cannot sit safely, like nothing is wrong.
When His little lambs are not where they belong.
So head to the highways, the byways, and hedges.
Climb mountain ridges and search right to the edges.
Those lambs they are out there, so keep moving on.
Do not give up from the dusk to the dawn.
Look up and look down, everywhere you go…
Keep your eyes peeled, Search high and search low.

We must keep searching, everywhere, anyhow.
The next one to be found could be waiting right now.
Out searching for souls, that's where I must be.
After all, that's what the Good Shepherd did for me.

Bats in the Belfry

I arrived at church just the other day.
I came through the doors in the usual way.
There were songs to learn, and time to pray.
I began to walk in the Christian way.

And I was talking to the pastor about what I might do, and he said, "Someday you can serve Him too, boy. Someday you can serve Him too."

And the bat's in the belfry, and guitar's out of tune. Sunday school picnics in the month of June.
"When can I serve the Lord? I don't know when…"
But they'll let me know right then, ya, you know they'll let me know right then.

I offered to help with the nursery class
Or wash the dishes or cut the grass.
"Do you need my help?" They said, "Not today."
"You're still too young." I said, "That's okay."

And the bugs in the soundboard, and the kitchen door creaks,
The baptismal tank is all full of leaks.
Do they need my help? Well they said they don't. I'd like to pitch in but I guess I won't.

So I went off to college just the other day
I came home for the summer and I had to say,
Hey there pastor, can I lend you a hand?
He said, "No, we're all good, everything's been planned."

I got a job and a wife and a kid or two
There were planes to catch and things to do.
I still love the Lord and my faith is sincere…
But I've got no time to volunteer.

And they've lost the cradle in the nativity…
And the star is missing from the Christmas tree.
"Who's going to help, well it won't be me…
I'm real busy, so just leave me be."

The pastor called me up just the other day
He said where you been brother? I said "I been away."
He said the youth need help with the Easter play.
I said, "I'm too old now, and all my hair's turned grey."

And as I hung up the phone it was plain to see…
Serving at the church was never habit for me.
It's not because I'm so cold-hearted,
I guess it's something that just never got started.

And the cast in the Christmas play all have the flu.
There's no one to serve the soup kitchen stew.
We need everyone to get on board.
Everyone has a place in the service of the Lord.

Note

Yes, this is the church version of "Cat's In the Cradle" by Harry Chapin. Years ago, I took songs I wrote into public schools to promote values and self-esteem, and a teacher said, "Wow, you're a real Harry Chapin, aren't you?" And I said, "Who?" Music is capable of telling great stories and conveying tremendous emotion, and this one reminds us that if we don't involve youth and children in our churches when they are young, they will not be there when they are older!

Lakeshore's Christmas float, 2020

Blest to Be a Blessing

Christmas is hectic and cluttered, filled with tinsel and dressing
But please don't forget: you're blest so you can be a blessing.
There are lights and parades, and shopping, eating and excessing…
But it's not about us… God has blest us so that we can be a blessing!
You can hop on a plane and travel the world, with your faith professing…
But when your feet touch the ground, find a way to be a blessing.
Are you hurried? Are you worn out? Are you harried and stressing?
Chillax, slow down…and take a moment to be a blessing.

When life goes too fast, and everything seems so pressing
Something happens when we pause and choose to be a blessing.
And when Christmas has passed, and you're slowly decompressing…
And you look back on it all, a frozen moment you are reassessing,
You won't think of yourself any the lesser
If you used your blessings to choose to be a blesser!

Candy

I will admit I am somewhat one-dimensional…
Though to some it seems somewhat unconventional
I am determined in all times and ways to be intentional.
I cannot be making stops for gumdrops and lollipops.
I do not want sweet tarts or candy hearts.
Keep your sweets and candy bars… I will not be fueling up on Mars.
Why are you offering gingerbread? Haven't you heard a word I've said?

The lust of the eyes shall not keep me from the prize.
Don't give me a hassle if I avoid your candy castle.
I won't be bogged down in mountain passes filled with chocolate or caramel or molasses.

I don't want butterscotch or fondue
I have places to go and things to do…
Intentionally I am pressing through.
Keep your cakes and baking and junk food parties…
I don't need Snickers or Aero, or KitKat or Smarties.

Those things will only delay and detour me
From reaching the destiny that God has for me.
In light of the evidence I think it only sensible…
I must keep my eyes on the prize and be totally intentional.
If you must know the truth I do have quite a sweet tooth
But let's say I stopped for peanut brittle,
Determined I'd have just a little
Before you know it, I ate a lot…
And a bellyache is what I've got!
Life is sweet, some would say…
But don't let sweets and treats get in your way.

Crunchy or crispy or ooey and gooey…
We don't need such distractions now do we?
I have a destiny, and I know God has plans…
I don't want it to melt away in my hands…
I scream that ice cream is really tasty good
But just because you can, does it mean you should?
Stop and snack for a while, I could, and I would…
But I've tasted and seen that God, He is good.
I'm seeking His best and this is indispensable…
I must be about my Father's business. I must be intentional.

Note

I included this piece in a sermon series called, "Candyland." While junk food is a problem to healthy eating, there are many *junk food* pursuits that get in the way of spiritual growth and maturity as well, so being intentional about saying no to spiritual *junk food* is part of growing in one's faith!

Coach Cliché

I know it feels like we're down and out. We're up against it. We've hit the wall. The walls are crumbling down. We're back on our heels. We're on the ropes. We've been backed into a corner. It's fourth and goal, and the clock has just run out… We're down to our last shot.

We're behind the eight ball. We're a day late and a dollar short. We're out of sync, and the score is out of reach. We've burned our last bridge. We've written cheques our bodies couldn't cash. We've dropped the ball one time too many. We're in over our heads. It was gut-check time, and we took one too many to the breadbasket. We got the short end of the stick and the long arm of the law. We ran into a buzz saw, and the whole thing is a train wreck. We're in the basement. We're out of their league. We are so bad, we're in a league of our own.

It was a slam dunk. We didn't have a chance. We didn't have a prayer. One, two, three strikes, we're out at the old ball game. It's all over but the crying because it's turned into laugher. There is no joy in Mudville as they look to drive the last nail in the coffin. It's time to warm up the bus for the long ride home because the wheels fell off the bandwagon. Turn out the lights, and start the long journey into night.

But wait…now just hold on there… Somebody rally the troops. Call out the dogs, and call off the hounds. Gentlemen, start your engines. Pull out all the stops, and batten down the hatches. Keep your eye on the ball, keep your stick on the ice, dip your toes in the water, and circle the wagons. It's time to step up to the plate…toe the line…take the field…hit the ice.

Because it ain't over till it's over… It might be the bottom of the ninth, and we're down to our last gasp, our last hurrah, our last kick at the can… Rumours of our demise have been greatly exaggerated. It doesn't get any better than this… it's all on the line.

Ding, ding, ding, we're answering the bell. Cinderella is trying on the glass slipper.

There's no I in team, but this team is in it to win it.

We've got more than a fighting chance… We're turning the tide.

It's rally time. The momentum has shifted. We're firing on all cylinders. We're off to the races. We're not pulling punches. This is a grand slam, slam dunk buzzer beater, a walk off, a knockout. It came down to the wire, and we're coming out on top. The doctor is in, and we're putting on a clinic.

What made the difference? It's when players become a team; when the *I* becomes we. It's when the doubts become belief; it's when the obstacles become opportunities; it's when the setbacks become stepping stones. It's when faith conquers fear… It's when we realise greater is he that is in me than he that is in the world.

I am more than a conqueror!

Pickle

Sometimes I change my mind, I'm uncertain and I'm fickle
But posilutely absotively…Lord, make of me a pickle.
Immerse me in Your Spirit, like a flood, not just a trickle.
Change and rearrange me, Lord, And make of me a pickle.
Up till now, I've hummed and hawed, and been somewhat non-committal
But I ask You now with all my heart to make of me a pickle.
All the things that I've pursued they are not worth a nickel.
They are gone, and it is on! Transform me into a pickle.
You've cut right through the things I knew, like a real sharp sickle
And shown me what my life can be, if I am willing to be a pickle.
Now I can't be sayin' if there'll be pain… Will it tickle or will it prickle?
I don't care I came prepared—to be changed into a pickle.
If pickle is the flavour and the savour that You want for me
Lord, dip me, dunk me, douse me, and a pickle I will be.

Note

I included this poem in a sermon in 2016 about the baptism in the Spirit. The Greek word translated *to baptise* has been defined as *immerse until changed*…as in, the process of pickling a cucumber.

A Multitude of Sins

I've always tried to live in such a way that everybody wins…
Boy am I glad that love covers a multitude of sins!
I've made my mistakes, I've been down and out, and kicked in the shins…
But what a relief that love covers a multitude of sins.
I'm sure we all get knocked down, with punches to our chins…
But that's okay, because love covers a multitude of sins.
I don't mean to complain…no need to strike up the violins…
But I just couldn't do this, if love couldn't cover a multitude of sins.
When evil has a field day, and the devil simply grins…
Somebody remind him that love covers a multitude of sins.
Covered by grace, washed in the blood, that's where ministry begins…
Thank you, Jesus, that love covers a multitude of sins.

Me in my Elvis jumpsuit

The Gospel According to Elvis

Well, since my baby left me, I've found a new place to dwell...
But it's not at the end of Lonely Street, because I've been welcomed into God's family now.

There was a time when I was *all shook up,* but now there is *peace in the valley for me.*

I was *caught in a trap,* with a *suspicious mind,*
But I put my *T-R-O-U-B-L-E* in an envelope marked *return to sender.*
When life started to *Shake, Rattle and Roll,* I just wanted to *make the world go away,*
But that's when you gotta *put your hand in the hand* of the man from Galilee.

I am no longer *cryin' in the chapel* now that the Lord is my *bridge over troubled waters. Viva,* Lord Jesus! Let the *jailhouse rock* all it wants because the *chain around my neck* is gone and I've been set free. I won't be cruel, I *ain't never caught a rabbit* and Jesus is a *friend of mine.*

And now, the end is near, I've reached the final curtain... And *if tomorrow never comes,* well...*that's alright, mama... that's alright with me.* You can have my *blue suede shoes...* because there's gonna *swing low a sweet chariot* coming forth to carry me home!

You can keep your *Blue Hawaii,* your *yellow rose of Texas,* and the *Green, Green Grass of Home,* because I'll be walking on streets of Gold. I've cancelled my reservations down at the *Heartbreak Hotel,* and I'm looking forward to a *mansion just over the hilltop.*

Note

Even though Elvis was considered the King of Rock and Roll music, the only three Grammy awards he won in his lifetime were all in gospel music.

Father of the Year

If you're looking for the perfect dad, There's really only One.
And He's always willing to adopt Another daughter or a son.
If you wonder if He loves you, Do not fret or fear
The Perfect picture of Parenting… He's the father of the year.
He has hands to help, and to hold, hands that are so strong
Hands that circle round us and tell us we belong.
He disciplines the ones He loves, I must make that clear
But that's just another reason why He's father of the year.

You might not get all you ask for, but I think you'll see
He gave us what we needed most at a hill called Calvary.
When we were far away He made a way to draw us near
What else can you say about the Father of the year?
We may say that we love Him, but it's at times insincere
But He doesn't ever love us less, He's the father of the year!
Sometimes we say, "You're not my dad, so don't you interfere!"
Wouldn't that be strange for the father of the year to hear?

Ignoring Him, we turn our back, to go through life alone…
But unwavering, He's always there, He never leaves His own.
At times, we get thrown to the ground, and we don't even know…
It is Him, all along, that gives us strength to grow.
As we pick ourselves up, there's a sound of a roaring cheer…
There in the stands proudly clapping His hands is the father of the year.
He's the Daddy of the decade, Best in a million years
And when I see Him face to face, He'll wipe away my tears.

What tears, you ask? The tears because I did not love Him more
That I doubted and I pouted, and forgot what life was for.
He'll run to me, and down on one knee, pull me into His embrace

And I'll know in that moment He's the father of life, and love and grace.
As He looks me in the eye, though I try to turn away,
He'll say, "Look at me, child." I have something I must say.
And I might expect chastising, or a condemning word…
But it's actually the most awesome thing I have ever heard.

He says, "Your heavenly rest awaits you, the war has been won;
We'll enter in together… Well done, my son, well done."

Fear not. Jump right in!

Fear Not!

F is for fears, and I've had my share.
Times when I've wondered, "God are You there?"
I believe God is faithful. I believe He is true.
But when life gets all crazy, what you gonna do?

E is exaggerate, for that's what fear does.
It blows trouble up bigger than it ever was.
Little things become a really big deal.
When fear takes over, that's how I feel.

A is anxiety and fretting and worry.
And times when I freeze up and times when I hurry.
Times when I feel like nothing goes rightly.
And it seems those times are daily and nightly.

R is for rainclouds hanging over my head…
Those days when I don't feel like getting out of bed.
I keep a brave face, but I must confess…
I can't keep up the race when life is a mess!

N is for normal, that's what I wish I was.
But I know I am not, and I know it's because…
Fear just takes over, yes, fear took control.
You no longer feel healthy, you no longer feel whole.

O is for oppression that makes human souls shrink.
It becomes an obsession quicker than one might think.
It pinches and squeezes until you're in chains.
It taunts and it teases and adds to your pains.

T is for trouble, I'm sure it's soon on the way.
It seems there's a new batch for each new day.
If only I could find some way out of here.
Some way to defeat the worry, and fear.

Aha… *F is for faith*…bigger than my fears!
Faith conquers darkness, faith quenches tears.
Faith is belief that there's coming a dawn…
And no matter what, my heart will go on.

E is for eternal…that's what my God is.
I am His child, forever I'm His.
I don't fear tomorrow, I won't fear today.
For I am His child and help's on the way.

A is for assurance beyond any doubt.
Assurance it is that kicks anxiety out.
"You cannot stay here, you fretting and fear…"
Assurance says, "Get that garbage outta here!"

R is for rest and sweet relaxation.
I lean on His arms and trust His salvation.
No weapon formed against me shall stand.
I rest and rejoice in the palm of His hand.

N is for now, because this is my time.
I may have lost ground but I'm ready to climb.
With an ironclad will and nerves of pure steel
I'm moving on with Jesus at the wheel.

O is for opportunity, and I will not cower.
He gives me wisdom and He gives me power
I renounce those fears they just cannot stay.
Whom shall I fear if God leads the way?

T is for the trust that I have in my God.
That should not surprise you, don't think it odd.
For no matter what, this one promise I've got
His word tells me plainly, Fear not! Fear not! Fear not!

This photo is a reminder that timing is everything!
And the perfect time is now!

God-time

Have you been running your toes through the sands of time?
It's time to clean your clock and synchronise your watches.

It's God-time, brother.

You might have thought you had all the time in the world…
But you can't just bide your time.
Nothing is frozen in time, and if you've lost track of time,

I'll tell you what time it is… It's God-time, sister.

In this world, Time keeps on ticking.
But don't just rock around the clock tonight. Make it count.
You're in the right place at the right time to turn over a new leaf,
And start barking up the right tree for a change.
Now is the time. You have a date with destiny.

It's game time. It's go time. It's God-time.

Live in the present. Live in the Presence; meaning, the Presence of God.
He calls you away from hustle and bustle, from the rat race and the wild goose chase.

It's God-time.

God-time is the time in His Presence.
He woos you to a place of rest, refreshment and rejuvenation.
His love is without end. His power is without equal.
His plans are with revision or correction. His wisdom is above rebuttal.

Though His ways be scrutinised, they can never be compromised, dismissed or trivialised. He stands alone above The corridors of time. And yet He invites You into intimacy.

He will refill your tank. He will recharge your batteries.
He will reset your compass. He will resharpen your axe.
He will renew Your strength. He will restore your passion.
You want to beat the clock? Step into God-time!

There's no time like the present.

There's no place like the Presence.

Picture-Perfect Marriage

If you want a picture-perfect marriage, it'll take some work
Marriage is like a camera, with one simple little quirk.
It does not come with autofocus, but no need to be scared
You can make it through this if you are prepared.

Take the time each day and get your spouse in your sights
And learn when to open windows and when to dim the lights.
Zoom in on the best things about your brand new spouse.
And filter out the bad stuff you don't want in your house.

Yes, we've all got our challenges, the women's and the men's.
But it doesn't help to seek them out with a telephoto lens.
If there's ever trouble between the two of you
Keep in mind the bigger picture, with a panoramic view.

Like editing of a photo, we've been given grace.
Forgiving one another is like retouch to a face.
Grace is like a trip to the mall to get some glamour shots
That covers up our blemishes, and all our blots and spots.

Once we've been exposed to God's grace in our lives
It should make us gracious as husbands and as wives.
Every day might not be picture-perfect, but that's okay.
May your marriage be a portrait of grace and love, we pray.

Note

This poem was shared in the wedding ceremony for a couple of photography buffs. I hope they learned to keep the *negatives* out of their life together!

Could You, Would You?

Could you—would you—meet with God,
In a place that might seem odd?
For church is not the only place
To know the Lord's warm embrace.

His presence can be real to you
In many other places too.
Wherever you go, He is there…
In fact, God is always everywhere!

Could you meet him in the rain?
Could you meet him on a plane?
Could you meet him on a cruise?
Can you pray in steel-toed shoes?

Could you meet God in the park?
Or on a bus or in the dark?
On a mountaintop or by the sea?
In a desert or up a tree?

Or in a store or in a box?
Or while you're wearing woolly socks?
In your house or out of doors
Or while you're mopping dirty floors?

Could you seek him on your knees?
Or in a tent at Lake Louise?
Could you praise Father, Spirit, Son?
While you're out, about, and on the run?

On the farm or at the zoo
Perhaps the Lord waits for you?
In the country or in the hood
Meet with God? I think I could…

The question is not "Could you?" but…"Would you?"

Pierced

All of the waiting, anticipating; The Child is on the way.
Pregnancy glow? It may not be so! But it seems this is the day!
The time finally comes, little fingers and thumbs, on this precious little Boy;
There is smiles and laughter, but not long after, a warning amid the joy:
"This child shall be special, this is true,
And a sword shall pierce your own soul too."

Just as Mary was told in those days of old, all mothers: be prepared!
Some days are good, hey, knock on wood! Other days ought not be shared!
From morning to night, when nothing goes right, mothering is a chore;
Kids go through phases, and though you're mad as blazes, could you ever wish for more?
Would you take on this task if you knew
That a sword may pierce your own soul too?

As the child grows, I'm sure everyone knows, kids listen to many voices.
You give them the tools, and try to set rules, but they'll make their own choices.
Love can be toughest when life is the roughest, For Momma/Mother/Moya/Mum.
Though love might be tested it will never be bested, no matter what trials may come!
What else is a caring mom to do,
Knowing a sword may pierce your own soul too?

Though tears may fall, it's a unique call, to fill a mother's role.
Moms need strong hearts for life's filled with darts, and piercings of the soul.
Moms can be weepy, for they love so deeply. Can it be any way other?
Most Moms would not trade, the price they have paid…to have the pierced soul of a mother.

Note

Inspired by our friend Moya who lost her son in 2017. *Moya* is a nickname for *mother* in some cultures. The "pierce your soul" quote is taken from Luke 2:35, where Mary is told baby Jesus will one day bring a piercing to her own soul, presumably referring to the pain she would feel at His crucifixion. And I've watched many moms experience a piercing of the soul when their child dies, or their child closes the door of relationship, or they choose a contrary path in life. Our Heavenly Father knows this pain well, and offers comfort. Take solace in Psalm 147:3, which says, God "heals the broken-hearted and binds up their wounds."

Give thanks for God's many blessings, especially for his amazing grace!

Grace...and It's Amazing!

His cross of death is our door to life.
His cross of solitude is our bridge to fellowship.
His cross of shame is our invitation to glory.
His cross of pain purchased our comfort and joy.
His cross was a bitter cup so we could taste the sweet goodness of God.
He took the full brunt of the law so we can know the liberating power of grace.
He was pierced so that we could be made whole again.
He allowed Himself to be weak, so that we could be strong.
He became poor so we could know the riches of God.
He became nothing so we could become everything God created us to be!
That is grace, and it's amazing.

Call it the Great Exchange, the deal of the century, the opportunity of a lifetime…
He's made us an offer we can't refuse…
We got the goods and He took the blame.
Its not too good to be true, but it's definitely too good to ignore.
We didn't ask for it, we'll never qualify for it, and we cannot possibly pay it back… but still He offers it. It's grace. And it's amazing.

Grace is greater than all our sin…in the same way that an ocean is greater than a raindrop.
Grace is without equal. Grace is beyond explanation.
Grace is a gift to beggars and to thieves, and to all of us who least deserve it.
Grace is grander than all the wildest dreams and clever contrivances of the human heart.
Grace grows higher as the river grows deeper.
Grace grows stronger when the mountains grow steeper.
And maybe just maybe…the reason we've been given it, is that we in turn might give it away.

How can I judge others when the King of Justice spoke grace over me?
How dare I pray punishment upon others when pardon was granted unto me?
I cannot leave others out knowing how Grace pulled me back in.

I dare not hold others down after the way Grace lifted me up.
Grace builds bridges, not barriers.
Grace is a palace, not a prison.
Grace allows relationships, not regulations.
With all of its other amazing properties, the most astounding thing about Grace might well be that the more you Share it with others, the more you yourself will come to enjoy.

Grace is to forgive, even when we find it hard to forget.
Grace is to let go, and let God.
Grace is to treat others as God has forgiven me.

That is grace…and what else can I call it but amazing?

Heavenly Minded

Too heavenly minded to be any good?
Yes, I'm focused on glory, but not as much as I should!
Heaven is not just for the dearly departed;
Eternal life has already started!

Too heavenly minded? That's not really a thing!
As in heaven, I want to live like Jesus is King.
Too heavenly minded? I don't think so…
May His will be done down here below.

I'm heavenly minded, but not just to visit;
Although I'm sure the décor is gloriously exquisite!
I'm setting my mind on things above…
Like holiness, praise, peace and love.

I'm heavenly minded, but not streets of gold,
Not pearly gates, Not to never grow old.
Those all sound good but just as in heaven
I want to honour Jesus 24/7.

I don't have the voice of an angel, that's true
But praising the Lord is what I was made to do.
I don't have a harp, and I don't have a cloud
But I'll praise him right now! I'll shout it out loud!

To be heavenly minded, this is the way
Praise and give thanks, trust and obey.
To be heavenly minded? I'll tell you how…
Live as if you are in heaven right now!

Heaven's Choir

If we could travel to that far-off golden shore
And walk together through heaven's open door
Can you imagine looking up even higher
Into the faces of an endless shining choir…
And what a sound as this choir boldly sings
Praises to the Lord of lords and King of kings.

What would possibly be our thoughts
As we search for our own spots…
Ah…there it is…that's the place for me.
Seat number 238, 423.
And hey, there's also a place for you…
Seat number 238, 422.

Let us join this triumphant throng
Boldly singing heaven's song…
But hey, don't wait, let's sing right now…
It's not hard, I'll tell you how…

We are not yet in heaven's crowd…
But we can sing His praises strong and loud…
Though life may have its ups and downs…
Someday we will cast down our crowns.

When we shall see that Glorious Lamb…
The Son of God, and the Great I Am…
But this is the day now and always
To exalt His name and raise the praise…

Let His praises be repeated!
Don't stay silent, and don't stay seated…

If you know what I'm talking about…
Stand up and give a hallelujah shout!

For worthy worthy worthy is the Lamb…
All praises to the Great I Am.

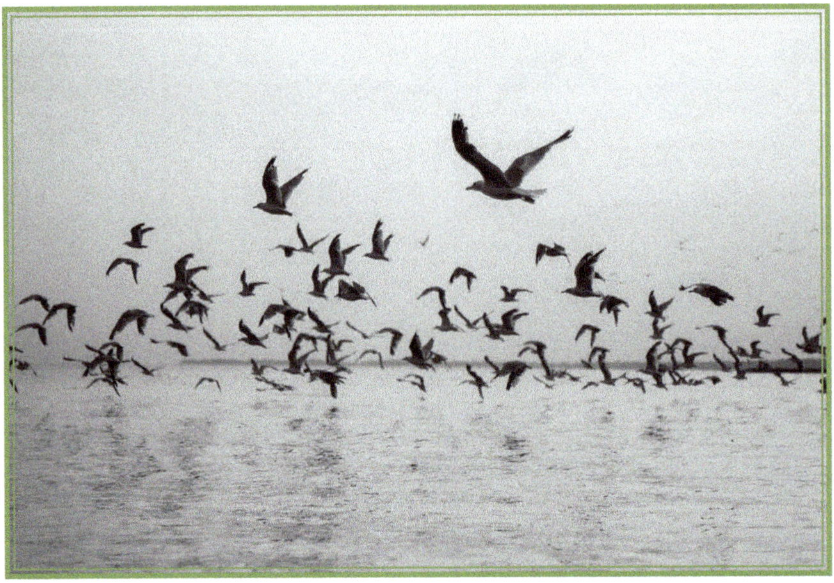

Beach Bum

If life is a beach as some people say
Then there'd be no more rent to pay
We'd all sit and wiggle our toes in the sand
I'd wax up my board and hit the surf
Wouldn't that be heaven on earth
And we'd call Californy the promised land!
We'd eat watermelon and corn on the cob
We'd never have to get another job
Wouldn't that be a California dream come true?
I'd sleep under the stars at night
And make sure my tan looks just right…
Maybe I could join the Baywatch crew?
I'd ride the waves and shoot the curls
Trimmed and toned to impress the girls
I'd learn the moves that make them scream and shout…
From dawn to dark I'd be hanging ten
Grab a little sleep then do it again,
Just don't say that dirty word… WIPEOUT!

I've been at the beach now for only a week
And everybody's treating me like a freak
I'd have to admit it's all my own fault;
You see, I just can't build a life out of sand
This just hasn't gone the way I'd planned
My dream has come to a grinding halt!

Bar-bar-bar, Barbara-Ann
Told me I'm no longer her man
Rhonda tried to help but she broke my heart;
The little deuce coupe is in the shop
My life as a surfer was a belly flop

My California dreams have fallen apart!
Surf City is just not for me
This isn't the place I want to be!

Note

    These are song lyrics I wrote for school presentations I did years ago on topics like values, antibullying, and achievement. This song—with its Beach Boys sound—was meant to encourage the students NOT to drop out of school and live on a beach somewhere but rather to apply themselves to their studies and achieve their dreams.

Flavour of Canada

Lord, help me bring Your flavour to this glorious land.
I want to serve You, but I cannot stand to be bland.
Let me live sweetly so as to touch others' hearts
Just like the raisins and pastries found in butter tarts.
Help me speak clearly, never stammer or stutter.
I'll keep to the task like I'm stuck on peanut butter.
Like French fries with gravy and cheese I am keen
To add some hot gooey goodness, just like poutine.
When opportunity knocks, please let me not spoil
Anoint me afresh, as with canola oil.
When I am tempted, my faith Lord, please stir up.
Help me stick to you just like maple syrup.
Lord whatever you do, whatever plans you are makin'
Let me sizzle and snap like Canadian back bacon.
And what do you say, do I have any takers?
Are you ready to be poured out of your shakers?
Give it all that you've got, with all that your worth
For we, my friends, are the salt of the earth.

Note

I shared this poem at a Canada Day event one summer, using a list of food items that had been created in Canada or at least strongly associated with Canada. And of course the reference to the salt of the earth reminds us all to live with the distinctive taste of *faith* in everything we do.

Last-Minute Shopping Blues

I hear shopping carts a-coming
Rolling through the mall
I try to stay out of their way
But I can't dodge them all.

Well I'm stuck here in this shopping mall, on Christmas Eve
There's people everywhere… Like you would not believe.

When I was just a young boy,
My momma told me, "Son…
Never wait till the last date
You'll never get it done."

Well I wish that I had listened, But now I walk these floors;
And I won't get my shopping done, before they close the stores.

My wife would like some fine china,
But all they had were coffee mugs
I went looking for some headphones
But they had only earplugs.

I went looking for a diamond ring
But all they had was brass.
And when I complained to the manager
All I got was sass.

I tried to buy a real nice dress,
But the sizes were all wrong
They only had one sweater left
But the sleeves were way too long.

The candy store was my last hope, but the chocolates were sold out
All they had left was a bag of Brussel sprouts.

Shopping for my lovely wife
Was so frustrating
'Cuz all the stores were empty
I couldn't find a thing.

I can only think of one gift
To put under our tree
I will wrap up myself
And I will give her…me!

Note

    A frantic Christmas tribute to "Folsom Prison Blues" by Johnny Cash.

Mmmm... From Los Puntos Cantina restaurant in Point Edward, Ontario

Don't Lose Yourself
(At the Buffet Table)

His palms are sweaty, his plate is heavy, third time at the buffet table already!
He eyes the spaghetti, tacos, nachos, big plate of apple betty.
But don't forget… Not time for dessert yet—
Green eggs and ham, Peanut butter and jam
Don't get in the way of this hungry man!
There's salad and borscht,
And of course, the main course,
He's going to eat like a horse.
He's spooning out a big load of chow—He's choking now.…
He's lost all reality
Oh, there goes gravity,
Pulling him down and he knows he'll have cavities
And it's sad but he goes back happily,
Eating the sweets and treats unflappably…
Cream puffs and pie crusts
Cherries, lemon and lime…
He's going back for seconds for the third and fourth time!

Don't lose yourself at the buffet table
You've got to be able to know when to say 'quit.'
You only got one pair of pants,
Do not take the chance
That if you don't quit, they won't fit…
Just say, "That's it!"

You call the waitress named Mabel over to the table,
I can't believe then you asked her for a menu…
Can't eat anymore, can you?
You've eaten three of everything from eel to veal,

What else can she bring to complete this meal?
You want the fettucine?
Or zucchini tortellini?
Fat-free sandwich spread
On the pumpernickel bread?
Crème brûlée and cheese soufflé,
Steaks and shakes and grape crepes…
Chicken legs and hard-boiled egg
Orange juice and chocolate mousse?
You want some chicken noodle
On top of cherry strudel?
How about the fish fillet?
It's really good, so they say…
You're in a mood for more food,
I know it…
Don't throw it up in my car;
Don't go too far!
You laugh at me, you gasp and wheeze,
As happily you look Mabel in the eye and say…
"Check, please!"

Don't lose yourself at the buffet table
You've got to be able to know when to say 'quit'.
You only got one pair of pants,
Do not take the chance
That if you don't quit, they won't fit…
Just say, "That's it!"

Note

  A parody of "Lose Yourself" by Eminem, that I used to sing in schools to encourage the exercise of self-control. I think my lyrics are much tastier than the original, although it does include a reference to Mom's spaghetti.

Go and Make Disciples

Go and make disciples… is the commission we've been given.
Tell them of salvation and the glories of His heaven.
Go and make disciples… that's the message we've been told
That they can be forgiven and walk on streets of gold.
Go and make disciples… please do not delay.
The whole world is waiting, and this could be the day.
Go and make disciples… it is the Lord's command.
Take the love of Jesus to every far off land.
From Sarnia to Mexico, Zimbabwe and Japan
To Russia, to Rwanda, to China and Peru…
Go and make disciples all the way to Timbuktu!
Freely we've been given it's ours to freely share…
Go and make disciples… Anytime, anyhow, anywhere!
Go and make disciples, till everyone can know…
Disciples of Jesus Christ… Go, Go, Go, Go, Go, Go!

Harold Will Sleep Tonight

Late one night,
Out for a drive,
Harold pulls in to a parking lot;
He never knew what his friends would do…
They had a gun, he heard shots!

Harold was told since he was 2 years old
The thing to do was 'tell the truth.'
But to his surprise
The other guys
Went to the judge and told lies!
Now Harold's in jail, his honesty failed.
But he still believes justice prevails…

Sticks and stones may hurt you
And words may slander your virtue
But if you've done what you knew was right
Harold you'll sleep tonight.

Day after day, life slips away.
He knows he told the truth
He still believes that he will be freed
If only he had some proof!

The day finally came,
The judge cleared his name.
Harold walked out the front door
His honour intact, He'll never be back
He's not the same anymore!

Sticks and stones may hurt you
And words may slander your virtue
But if you've done what you knew was right
Harold you'll sleep tonight.

Note

 Based on the true story of Harold Morris, wrongfully convicted of murder after a liquor store shooting in the 1970s. Harold became a born-again Christian in jail and wrote his story in a book called *Twice Pardoned*. This was a song I sang in public school classrooms to encourage integrity, truthfulness, and virtue. Virtue was a word I had to define for the students, as it has fallen out of use in our world. And out of practice as well, largely.

No Secret

In case you ever wondered where you stood with Annette…whether she was secretly sizing you up, discreetly looking you over, or whether she might actually be straight up counseling you without you even knowing it…

If she ever asked you, "And how did that make you feel?", you might have been a client.

If she ever said, "So what would that look like in your situation?", you also might have been a client.

If she ever said, "Tell me what's new in your world," you were literally THIS CLOSE to being a client.

If you were ever seated at her dinner table for a meal, you felt like you were part of her inner circle (although you may not have been *in* on all the inside jokes).

If you ever told her about the mountain in your way, she left you with the profound and certain assurance that the mountain could be moved, tunneled under, climbed over, or camped upon.

If you ever unpacked your most intimate problems to her and looked up to see her warm smile and twinkling eyes, you knew you were heard, valued, and loved.

If you ever overheard her praying for you, you knew that she believed in a loving and potent God Who hears every word, and that she could almost see the light at the end of your tunnel getting brighter.

And if you ever had her call you "Pastor," well…you felt blest, you felt honoured, and you were deeply humbled. (I should know.)

No secrets here. No hidden agenda. She never camouflaged her concern for others; she wore it on her sleeve. And if you think she was nefariously snickering about you, don't sweat it; she laughed most and hardest at herself!

Though she kept confidences, she never kept secret how she felt about the people in her life.

Note

Annette and I worked together at Lakeshore Community Church from 2007 to 2013, when she and her husband Jim started a counselling ministry called Life's Seasons. She was a very dear and close friend. Passing into eternity in January 2020, it's no secret that Annette is now in the presence of her Saviour; but her legacy lives on. May we all learn what it is to live with three things that Annette modeled: the same dependence on God, a genuine concern for others, and the commitment to find and fulfil the purpose for which we were put on this earth.

Sarnia's iconic landmark, the Bluewater Bridge
(connecting to Port Huron, Michigan)

The Last Word

When it comes right down to your last word,
Would you say life is joy? Or is it absurd?

When you've come down to the last of the cup
Is there one last word that will sum it all up?

What is that word? What would it be?
Is there a word that's just right for me?

Is it "Goodbye," or just a "farewell for now"?
You could say, "Loved," because was I? Oh wow!

You could say, "Truthful," as in, my life was no lie.
You could say, "Blest," for if anyone was, it was I.

But "Amen" is the word that I have chosen with care;
(It's more than the "caboose" at the end of a prayer).

It's more than cliché, or a trite expression.
It's affirmation, confirmation, and confession.

The word "Amen," means, "So be it, I agree."
I hope that's the word they say about me.

Amen to the way that I tried to live.
Amen to the things I so wanted to give.

Amen to the faith that filled all of my days.
Amen to the volume I used to give praise.

Amen to the love that I tried to express.
Amen to the way I managed stress and duress.

Amen to the humour, the joy and the laughter;
Amen to high hopes in a happy ever after.

Amen to forgiveness, and grace greater than sin;
Amen to believing we can hold on for the win!

We don't live here forever, some day we move on.
And there will come a day when you hear I am gone.

Whenever that is, and wherever you are at,
I hope you'll smile and say "Amen. Amen to that!"

Not "Amen, he is gone," but "Amen to his story."
That I lived as I did, and to God be the glory!"

About the Author

Troy Tobey was born in Galt, Ontario—a town that no longer exists! He went to Eastern Pentecostal Bible College in Peterborough and graduated with a bachelor's degree in theology.

In the churches he has served in, he had, at various times, taken on the roles of youth pastor, children's pastor, senior pastor, Sunday school bus driver, and rock star.

In his leisure time, he enjoys sports, comedy, music, and long walks.

He lives near the beach in picturesque Bright's Grove, Ontario with his wife Kathleen. Together they have three grown children, Josiah, Lauren, and Micah. Serving as pastor of Lakeshore Community Church gives him opportunity to share his passion for the Christian faith and his unique brand of poetic creativity.

Lightning Source UK Ltd.
Milton Keynes UK
UKHW021415081022
410100UK00010B/235

9 781639 610556